FAITH'S REWARD

FAITH'S REWARD

DANIEL EPLEY

TATE PUBLISHING
AND ENTERPRISES, LLC

The opinions expressed by the author are not necessarily those of Tate Publishing, LLC.

Published by Tate Publishing & Enterprises, LLC
127 E. Trade Center Terrace | Mustang, Oklahoma 73064 USA
1.888.361.9473 | www.tatepublishing.com

Tate Publishing is committed to excellence in the publishing industry. The company reflects the philosophy established by the founders, based on Psalm 68:11,
"The Lord gave the word and great was the company of those who published it."

Book design copyright © 2013 by Tate Publishing, LLC. All rights reserved.
Cover design by Ronnel Luspoc
Interior design by Jomel Pepito

Published in the United States of America

ISBN: 978-1-62510-501-1
1. Religion / Christian Life / Spiritual Growth
2. Religion / Christian Life / General
13.02.06

CONTENTS

FOREWORD

In *Faith's Reward*, we find a message needed today by the community of God. In the midst of global turmoil, economic unrest, and the stressful setting of modern society, this book provides a source of strength and encouragement. I have known and been friends with Dan Epley for over thirty years. We both having pastored in the same city have grown up in the ministry together. As I read over this book, the thing that I was most excited about was the fact that Pastor Epley has lived and modeled these principles of faith. I have watched his life and observed his manner of confident trust in God. The rich collective wisdom of his years in ministry provides an insightful approach to faith that is drawn and built upon the biblical text. His experience in living out these faith principles is interwoven into the fabric of the printed page. The reader will be able to understand the many aspects of faith; this includes the kinds of faith, how faith operates, how faith is released in one's life, mindset of faith, dynamics of faith, faith and love, and living in the anointing. In short, it provides a thorough conceptualization "of faith in God" (Heb 6.1b, NIV). This book is a must-read for the person is who is ready to move forward in their own spiritual development. It consists of an easy to follow outline of topics that could be used in small-group studies, classes, personal devotions, and sermons. The Hebrews writer states that "without faith it is impossible to please God…" (Hebrews 11.6a, NIV). Faith is essential in our spiritual formation. This book will tell you how to get faith, and most importantly it will show you how to live by faith.

J. Michael Brown, D.Min (Cand.), Gordon-
Conwell Theological Seminary
Senior Pastor
Crossroads Assembly
Asheville, NC

PREFACE

VICTORY IN JESUS

Have you ever found yourself backed into a corner by circumstances and wondered how you were going to get out? Has it ever seemed the whole world was positioned against you? I think we have all stood in that place at one time or another. While there may be a myriad of reasons we find ourselves in the situation, there is one biblical fact that remains a constant. Through faith in Christ, we are more than conquerors by Him who loves us.

There is an overcoming victory resident within our faith in God's Word. Ten lepers met Jesus on the road to Jerusalem. They cried out to Him for mercy and to heal their sick-ridden bodies. Jesus told them to go show themselves to the priest. He was giving them direction to lay claim to what they believed about Him and walk it out. He pointed them to victory. The scripture in Luke 17:14 said they were cleansed as they went. This would indicate these ten lepers experienced a progressive healing with every step of believing as they journeyed to the priest's home.

There are times in our life that we find ourselves engaged in a battle that grows more intense as time passes by. While the battle may seem to intensify, we have to set our attention on victory instead of defeat. We have to summon the courage and hope to see beyond the chaos and grief to declare the victory Jesus gained for us.

The Bible says that as believers, our faith contains the victory that overcomes this world. Every instance and provision we have and will ever need has been worked out for us by our eternal Father. He has given us this blessing within His Word. When we establish the Word of His grace into our hearts and minds, our faith becomes the substance of these things He has provided.

Everything—and I mean everything—is ready for us to withdraw from God's treasury. It has already been placed in our account. We often are caught waiting on God to do something when He is waiting on us to say something. All of the victory we will ever need has already been given to us. Peter tells us that we have been given exceeding, great, and precious promises, while the Apostle Paul says every thread making up the fabric of our victory is expressed to us through our Lord Jesus Christ.

This book places a great deal of emphasis on God's Word. In today's world of question, uncertainty, and unbelief, we can experience deliverance from the works of despair and destruction by placing the words of the Bible first place in our minds. I have listed several scriptural references that I encourage you to look up and study. God has revealed Himself to us within the pages of the Bible, and the Holy Spirit is more than ready to provide wisdom and understanding of the Scriptures. If we will take the time of getting to know Him through His Word, we will find freedom from much of the grief, sorrow, and pain that is around us today.

INTRODUCTION

This book is a culmination of sermons I have preached over the span of more than thirty years. It is the collective work of my heart and ministry. I believe the subject of faith is among the most important courses of study the church should engage in. I have found it to be one of those subjects that require continual attention because of the growing and changing characteristics of its nature. As we study Hebrews 11, we see God working in the lives of ordinary people through their faith. In reading their personal accounts, we discover the secret each of them shared is trusting in the Word of God. I can attest to the fact that our ability to trust is a developing and growing adventure.

Hebrews 11:6 is what I believe to be one of three keys that unlock the wisdom of Scripture. In this verse, we uncover the one thing that is at the core of the human experience, and that is to live pleasing to God. This desire has been placed into us as a center of our existence and acts like a directional guidance system leading and drawing us to the father heart of God.

This verse begins by saying, "Without faith, it is impossible to please Him." As a key, it reveals two truths about faith that plunge us into the delight of living a life that is pleasing to our creator. The cravings of our desire to live pleasing to Him are met as we understand that our identity is found in knowing Him.

FIRST TRUTH

The first truth is found in the phrase "He who comes to God must believe that He is." The most important application of our faith is knowing God for who He is. We often think first about what He has done or will do for us. Yet the first and most significant operation of our faith is searching the heart of God for who He is. This is where our identity is discovered for we are created in His image and likeness.

Before Moses could go into Egypt proclaiming to Israel their God had delivered them, he realized there was a need to introduce them to Him by name. So his question to God was, who shall I say sent me? This question is a reference to the fact we all need to know Him personally. As we grow in the depth and intimacy of our relationship with God, we arrive at convictions of who He is. It is from these convictions of faith we receive from Him.

SECOND TRUTH

The second truth is stated in the latter part of verse 6, saying, "And that He rewards them who seek [diligently, sincerely, and earnestly] for Him." Because it is God's desire to love us, He has embedded a reward within our passionate desire to know Him. This reward manifests in our lives based upon what we believe.

This truth identifies God as one who is positioned to bless all who belong to Him through Christ. Whatever and however His reward is identified in our life, it comes from the treasuries of His desire and purpose to reveal His goodness in every affair that has to do with us. In Matthew's gospel, Jesus said the Father's reward is not deceitful but that of goodness. As soon as we move toward God through faith, He moves toward us with more than we can ask or think.

With the application of these two truths, it is evident that this is how our faith operates. It searches out to know Him. As we enter the relationship of knowing Him, our faith releases the reward of God's person into our lives. There is no higher or nobler use of our faith than to exercise the privilege of drawing near to Him. Because of His promises to us, we are never separated from His great love.

Section 1

NOW FAITH IS...

THE THREE REALMS

As bible believers we embrace the Genesis account of creation as it is recorded that God created the heavens and earth. During this majestic and authoritarian act, we find Him dressing the Garden of Eden to be suitable for the part of creation which would bear His own image and likeness. This is not to say that humanity resembles God in outward appearance, but it is the inward appearance which is referenced in this statement. As God is a triune being within one identity, He created man to bear this same image and likeness. In doing so, God created man's body from the dust of the earth, yet the body continued to be lifeless until God imparted into His creation the essence of Himself, the breath of life. Then man became a living being.

At that moment God's created companion consisted of three components which are distinct in nature yet harmoniously knit together for singular function and identity. These components are the human body as it was created to be an earthly housing for the human spirit and soul.

Throughout the bible we are identified as a man consisting of a spirit expressing ourselves through a soul while living in a body.

In God's design and purpose for our creation, it was vital that His companion be created with the ability to occupy both environments; the heavenly which is spiritual and the earthly which is natural. Since death was not a part of the original design, God's intent was to pour Himself into the natural through the spiritual companionship He enjoyed with Adam. We see this fully accomplished through Christ who is referred to as the second Adam. The bible says in Second Corinthians that "God was in Christ reconciling the world to Himself." This portrayal of purpose continues to be seen today as Christ occupies the life of everyone born again with the ability to fulfill the Father's mission. This mission is identified within the prayer Jesus taught, specifically speaking of His will being accomplished in the earth as it is in heaven.

This is the reason God created man's body first. This wondrous housing has been given to us for earthly habitation. In Second Corinthians chapter 5, our body is identified as an earth suit. Without it, the spirit of man cannot stay here in this environment. Now we can understand the mystery of the Body of Christ. As God is omnipotent, yet He has instituted operational laws that impose the parameters of order which even He must live by. Therefore He dwells within the spirit of believers operating through their faith releasing His eternal purpose into the earth.

There is something else I want to mention here. The order created by the operational laws prevents us from occupying the earthly realm after our death. On several occasions we find scriptural reference to man's spirit and soul being separated from the body and immediately located in either heaven or hell. Jesus speaks of the rich man in Luke's gospel who died and immediately found himself in hell and likewise the beggar who was immediately in the comfort of paradise. The apostle Paul said "to be absent from the body is to be present with the Lord." We see this law in effect during Satan's temptation of Eve in the Garden of Eden. He required the cooperation of the serpent in order to engage Eve. You see, the body is the faculty of authority to have dominion in the earth. That's the reason Satan is constantly looking to occupy man's faculties so he can exercise dominion. It is the part of us which gives our spirit and soul the ability to exercise the rights of occupation as commissioned in Genesis 1:28.

Upon becoming a Christian we are born of God as a new creation and are restored to the image of the Father through the Son. In this restoration we discover ourselves once again capable of communing with God in companionship while taking our position as appointed by our Father to exercise dominion in the place we have been commissioned to occupy.

During the time of our occupation of this world, there are three realms we have contact with. They consist of the heavenly realm, the earthly realm, and the worldly realm. The worldly realm can also be referred to as the natural realm. We find biblical reference to the heavenly realm in Ephesians 1:3. *This realm is the home of the Kingdom of Heaven and the Throne of God.* It is normally invisible to our natural sight and exists beyond the contact of our senses. The subject concerning this realm is evident in the book of Genesis. From all indication, the heavenly realm and the earthly realm were to be in such agreement that God and man could fellowship by seamlessly passing from one to the other. There is evidence in the Scripture that these two realms were to be the world of reality that the natural realm would operate from. Jesus gave us this picture in the Gospels. Once again, the three realms are bridged and blended by the person of Christ Himself.

THE HEAVENLY REALM

As we study the life of Jesus and observe His interaction with the worldly realm, we can see the possibilities of faith. He is our pattern and mentor. I believe He modeled every situation along with the response needed to govern and advance the Kingdom of God. In John 14:12, He said that we would do the same things He did, getting the same results He experienced. He told us the key to this is believing in Him.

It is in the heavenly realm we have been blessed with all spiritual blessings in Christ. We access and live in this realm through faith in God's Word. The promises given to us grant us the privilege to partake of the divine nature of this realm. Upon Jesus' baptism, John witnessed the heavens open, and the Holy Spirit descended to rest upon Jesus. This marks an event where the heavenly realm invaded the earthly and

worldly realms. This event
the baptism in the Holy Spi
came to abide in the Body of C
of the Kingdom would reside in
intended in the Garden of Eden.

THE EARTHLY REALM

The second realm is what I am going to call the earthly realm. Jesus talks about the new birth and being born of the Spirit in John 3:3–12. He calls the spiritual activity of the new birth earthly things. Yet this is certainly spiritual in nature. This realm is relative to the visible earth yet still unseen and includes the atmospheric heavens. *Activity in this realm influences the visible earth and its affairs as we know it. This is the realm where angels and demons operate.* In Genesis 28:12, Jacob saw the angels of God ascending and descending. It is from this realm angels influence events and people in order to minister salvation to God's people. As the wilderness season for Jesus came to an end, Luke's gospel says that angels came and ministered to Him.

Jesus said, "When an unclean spirit is cast out, it finds itself in dry places without expression and rest. Then he says I will return to my house from which I came." The dry places mentioned here are in the earthly realm. The house referred to is the person's life from which the unclean spirit was cast out.

In Daniel 10:11–13, we find the struggle for influence and authority. This struggle involves heaven's archangels and one identified as the prince of the kingdom of Persia. This is most certainly a demonic

sought to rule through Cyrus, the king of
...ia. This conflict took place in the earthly realm.
It is this realm that we often describe as the spiritual
atmosphere in a place.

THE WORLDLY REALM

We find mention of the worldly realm in Luke 4:5–6.
Remember, as previously stated, the worldly realm and
natural realm are synonymous terms referring to the
same thing. Because of Adam's sin, the worldly realm
was delivered over to Satan's lordship. During Jesus'
temptation, we hear Satan offering Jesus this lordship
over the kingdoms of this world and their influence.
This is a genuine temptation because of Jesus' rebuttal.
The worldly realm is made up of controlling influences
resulting from the interaction of ruling attitudes.
According to the gospel of Luke, these attitudes are
under the authority of Satan who Jesus identified as
the god of this world system as well as a liar, deceiver,
thief, murderer, oppressor, and destroyer. This is the
devil's character, and this world system consists of these
characteristics. People have often become confused
because they believe God is responsible for everything
that happens. This thinking imposes a limit to what
God wants to do because it creates an inner struggle
concerning God's ability and willingness. The things
going on in this world that follow along the path of
these characteristics are not of God's doing. Yet He has
provided a salvation, which encompasses deliverance
from every situation, and this salvation is available to
all who will believe in His Word. Even in the bigger

picture, we may experience a bombardment of things we don't understand, yet we can trust God's overall control that He is working all things out for our good according to what we have believed. An example of this is in Mark chapter 5. We find a father desperately searching for Jesus, asking Him to come to his home because his daughter was sick in bed dying. This loving father knew that if could get to Jesus everything would be alright. His approach to Jesus would be synonymous with praying and Jesus agreed to come and heal her. Because they were detained for a while longer, the tragedy this father most greatly feared happened. He heard the news from his home that his daughter had died. His hope sank and fear gripped his heart. Even though he had believed, prayed, and received the promise from God, it didn't appear that things would turn out as he had hoped. When Jesus heard this report, he said to the father, "Fear not only believe." Jesus encouraged him to continue embracing the hope he had begun with. The rest of the story turns out just as the believing father had expected. This is an example of how God continues to work in our lives even though it appears we are lost in the sea of helplessness.

It has been validated over and over that the greater the platform of exposure we as believers attain, the greater the opposition to our effectiveness we experience. A reason for this is we engage in the challenge for influential leverage of the society and culture around us. In our own way, each of us occupies a slice of this world. This occupation also relates to our desire for growth and increase. The greater the influence you gain, the stronger the demonic resistance you experience. Jesus declares to us in the parable of the talents that we are destined for growth and increase. *God has seeded this anointing to increase within our faith, so He has already given us the authority to overtake, overcome, and occupy.*

The Bible says in 1 John 5:4, "This is the victory that overcomes the world, even our faith." The Word of God also says in 1 John 4:4, "Greater is He who is in us than he who is in the world." So in combining these two scriptures, we once again discover God's master plan to supplant Satan's hold on this realm as He uses us to revenge all disobedience and oppression.

TWO MIND-SETS

Our contact with the worldly realm requires, for the most part, an interaction with our senses. We engage this realm by smelling, touching, hearing, seeing, and tasting. This contact, engagement, and understanding are what I'm going to call the sensual mind. An example of this mind-set is found in God's first man, Adam. After Adam sinned, we find him aware of his condition of nakedness, which would indicate a shift of how he related to the world around him. This reveals that Adam's operational awareness is from the outside in. The Spirit of revelation was no longer connecting Adam to the God realm. His abilities to connect to the world around him were now processing through his five senses. This awareness has become our law of contact and is operational from the outside in. When we are influenced by stimuli resulting from the actions and circumstances of this world, its influences are allowed to control us. As we have discussed, faith in God's Word gives us liberty, freedom, and victory over the powers controlling this realm.

Our contact with the other two realms that cannot be seen with our natural eyes is by faith. Paul said in 2 Corinthians 4:18 and 5:7 that we walk in the unseen realms by faith and not by sight. I'm calling this mind-set the faith mind. This mind-set utilizes an operational awareness that is from the inside out. It is not influenced or persuaded by what is apparent but by what is believed and spoken. The Bible says of Abraham that he was fully convinced God would do what He had promised.

There came a time when Abraham was not in faith. In Genesis 15, we learn of an encounter between Abram and God that would shift Abram back over into a believing attitude. God changed the imagery of what he was looking at so his mind-set would change. Genesis 15:6 (NLT) says, "Abram believed the Lord and He counted him as righteous because of his faith." What was it that God said that had such an impact on Abram? In connection with the imagery, God told him, "So shall your descendants be."

The Bible says the sensual mind is in continual conflict with the faith mind. As two pole magnets resist one another, so the sensual mind is contrary to faith. It polarizes everything in our mind-set to resist and repel the things of God. This mind-set lives in connection with this present world. The Bible identifies the nature of this world paradigm as evil, and it is under the influence of the wicked one. So because of the sensual mind's alliance with the world, it too becomes susceptible to the governing influence of the ruler of this world.

So as a believer, the need is great that we develop our faith mind so we may discover the blessing, peace, and joy

God has given to us in Christ. It was Thomas, one of the twelve who lived with Jesus for over three years, who made the statement to the other disciples after Jesus death: "Unless I place my finger into his scars and my hand into his side, I will not believe." Thomas was allowing his ability to believe to be ruled by what he was able to validate with his eyes.

As discussed before, this is the sensual mind, and it is ultimately under the control of manipulating information, which affects us. You see, this mind must be renewed and changed into a faith mind. Paul said to the Roman church in Romans 12:2 (NLT), "Don't copy the behavior and customs of this world, but let God transform you into a new person by changing the way you think. Then you learn to know God's will for you, which is good and pleasing and perfect."

Thus, our thinking should not be conformed to this world but transformed to focus and understand the mind of Christ so that the unseen Kingdom of God can come into this world.

Jesus, being concerned with Thomas believing in Him, offered him his hands, feet, and side. Thomas believed by seeing Jesus' appearance and hearing His voice. Then Jesus made a defining statement: "Thomas, because you have seen me, you have believed. Blessed is those who have not seen and yet they believe." The Greek word translated providing us the word *blessed* in the English text means "to be empowered to prosper, a state of happiness, over-the-top blessed."

We can choose the attitude Thomas exhibited or the attitude Jesus declared. The attitude Jesus described carries the blessing. The need to see before we believe doesn't carry any blessing with it. We may experience a miracle, but our relationship with God doesn't grow. With a believing attitude, we not only receive from Him, but our relationship of knowing Christ also increases. Within this relationship, we experience the joy and confidence faith brings.

FAITH IS KNOWING GOD

The subject of faith in God is not just to obtain the promises that we may live the victorious life; it is also first and foremost the lifestyle of the Holy Spirit. Living in faith is the criteria for knowing Him in a more personal and powerful relationship. Christ dwells in our heart through faith. We will walk in a deeper communion with Jesus and experience a greater fellowship with God if we live in agreement with Him through faith in His Word.

Moses called out to God to reveal Himself so that he could know God in a new way. When we read this scripture in Exodus 33 out of the Amplified Bible, the word *know* is expanded upon to show Moses saying, "That I may progressively become more deeply and intimately acquainted with you." Moses's prayer indicates His passionate cry for a fresh revelation of God Himself. It is only from within his faith he could cry out to know Him in a way that was beyond his revelation and experience. It was by his faith he embraced this revelation and walked in it.

Paul revealed this same passionate cry as he exposed his primary desire while writing the letter to the Church at Philippi. He used this same phraseology in chapter 3 when he stated, "That I may know Him." In reading this passage from the Amplified Bible, we find Paul echoing Moses's prayer to progressively become more deeply and intimately acquainted with Christ while perceiving and understanding the wonders of His person more strongly and clearly. Moses and Paul alike experienced the overwhelming desire to know Him more.

Once we have tasted the fruit of this desire, our appetite for God continues to reach out for this deeper intimacy and knowledge of Him. *Every aspect of our sensory perception is taken to a new level of thrill, ecstasy, and depth of understanding when we encounter God's presence.* The writer of the book of Hebrews teaches that for us to come to God, we must believe that He is. It is from within this pursuit we know Him and come to Him. The reward pledged to the diligent is also evident to be the focus of our believing, that we shall grasp another glimpse and taste of His Glorious Person.

We are spiritually wired to commune with God at the highest level. The reference to "things" mentioned in 1 Corinthians 2:9–10 are mysteries and truths God has prepared for us. While this reference could infer the hope of our future in heaven, the most likely application of this passage is for the purpose of God continually revealing Himself to us by the Holy Spirit.

These mysteries and truths are wrapped up in God's Word for us to discover by the help of the Spirit so that we may know the blessing God has freely given to us.

As the Spirit who is in us speaks and cries out to the Father, we discover our role in this endeavor of searching out the inner depths of the Father's heart. As we yield to His voice and give articulation to His desire through prayer, we engage the privilege and access He has to the Father. It is here our role as a contact point comes into reality.

When something is revealed to us, it is also released to us. The drive, passion, and obsession we have for the Presence of God is Him drawing us into Himself by the Spirit. He wants us to walk with Him in His realm, perceiving and receiving His ways so that we may increase in our intimate knowledge of Him. Entering His realm is accomplished through three practices, which are the following: renewing our mind in His Word, spending time ministering to the Lord in prayer and praise, and being sensitive, faithful, and obedient to the moods, desires, and leading of the Holy Spirit.

We have the privilege of studying the behaviors and experiences of ordinary men and women as they pursued their passion for the greatness of God's love and person. It's a worthwhile study to see the overlapping practices of prayer and meditation in the lives of these people. This lifestyle enabled them to experience the magnificent intervention and invasion of God's wonderful presence and grace.

We also have opportunity to view through scripture the life and relationship of Christ He demonstrated during his earthly walk with the Father. This relationship exhibited by Christ has been made available to us through faith in Him.

THE GOD KIND OF FAITH

Jesus told His disciples in Mark 11:22 to "have faith in God." The marginal rendering in most study Bibles have the literal translation saying "have the faith of God" or the "God kind of faith." Jesus demonstrated this God kind of faith by first exercising authority over creation, namely the fig tree. His actions declared the God kind of faith superior to all other authority. One might reply, "Well, that's Jesus who created all things. Sure He can exercise authority over creation." While that is true, yet He said for us to have the same faith He was operating through while on earth. When God gave Adam dominion over all life on this planet, He was saying, "Adam, rule over your environment." The only life not mentioned within the sphere of Adam's dominion is human life. We do not have ruling authority over other people.

Otherwise, whatever is in your sphere is subject to your faith. Jesus implied the same thing in Mark 11:23 when He instructed the disciples to speak to the mountain, not doubting but believing that what they said would come to pass. In these instructions, He is teaching that we can rule over our environment through words spoken from the God kind of faith. These words carry the same dominion as was given to Adam.

As we survey every area of our life, we find situations and circumstances where our words of faith have influenced the outcome of those situations, resulting in victory. We also find some areas that require our attention. It is a best practice to meditate in God's Word in order to restore our mind in the authority of Christ. This should be done before we start out to subdue and bring change to those areas through our confession of the word of God and the prayer of faith.

Jesus said that through believing, we would possess what we say. I have always known when I was in faith because I was aware of the absolute authority to declare the biblical promise in Jesus' name. It is Jesus working through our faith, but it is our attitude of authority that releases the substance of Jesus. That's what He meant in John 14:14 when He said, "Ask anything in my Name and I will do it." The word for *ask* used in this passage of scripture is too strong for the idea of petition alone. It means requesting with authority while placing a demand on the resources available. Let's look at two statements further discussing the God kind of Faith.

AN ATTITUDE OF FAITH

An attitude of faith is characterized by that of believing and discovery. Jesus said all things are possible to him who believes. The reason I say believing is an attitude is because we choose to believe and embrace a possibility. Abraham chose to believe as God spoke to him concerning his posterity being as numerable as the stars of the sky.

The Bible says that while everything around him looked impossible, he believed God, and righteousness was accounted to him. Jacob chose to believe as he embraced the promise of returning to the land of his fathers. Joseph chose to believe that one day his people would leave Egypt. Moses chose to believe that he would lead Israel out of slavery as he was apprehended by God at the burning bush. Ruth chose to believe that there was a future and a hope while setting out to discover a destiny that was beyond her dreams.

These are but a few examples of everyday people who chose to believe and discover the great and vast future God had given them. The Bible is full of character stories concerning people like Gideon, who, being insignificant to culture and world events around him, chose to believe and accomplish the impossible.

Each of these men and women made a decision to embrace the role God placed them in releasing a torrent of heaven's power. They chose to enforce the authority of faith. From the action of their choices, God ignited a firestorm that altered history while charting the purpose and plan of His redemptive mystery.

The list goes on and on, and yet all the things they accomplished points to those of us who are at the end of the race completing the course. The firestorm continues to burn as the revelation of God's continued mystery is contained in our attitude to believe. There is yet much to discover. As each one of us choose to believe, we bring into experience the fullness of His grace in our time. It is our destiny to alter history while shaping the future for the next generations to live in the manifestation of heaven's culture.

FAITH IS THE SUBSTANCE OF THE KINGDOM

Faith is the substance of grace, which is the materiality of an unseen world known as the Kingdom of Heaven. Since Jesus said His Kingdom was not of this world, it is accurate to determine His Kingdom exists in the unseen realm. Jesus instructed His disciples as well as all who believe in Him to pray these words: "Your Kingdom come, your will be done on earth as it is in heaven." So Jesus taught us that this unseen world is accessible through prayer. If we combine this with Mark 11:24, we discover that this unseen world, which we have earlier identified as the heavenly realm, is accessible and touchable through the prayer of faith.

We understand God's grace to contain great promises through which we are delivered from the death-doomed behaviors that are characteristic of this present evil world. The more troubling the world becomes with sin and oppression, the greater His grace abounds toward us. If we receive God's grace by believing what he says, we take possession of a mixture of God's purpose and His power to bring His good pleasure to pass.

> God's law was given so that all people could see how sinful they were. But as people sinned more and more, God's wonderful grace became more abundant.
>
> Romans 5:20 (NLT)

God saved you by his grace when you believed. And you can't take credit for this; it is a gift from God.

Ephesians 2:8 (NLT)

For I am not ashamed of this Good News about Christ. It is the power of God at work, saving everyone who believes—the Jew first and also the Gentile.

Romans 1:16 (NLT)

Let's look at Hebrews 11:3 in the Amplified Bible: "By faith we understand that the worlds [during the successive ages] were framed (fashioned, put in order and equipped for their intended purpose) by the word of God, so that what we see was not made out of things which are visible." In this verse of scripture, we see the Word of God performing three functions as heaven comes to the earth.

1. The Word fashioned or created the worlds. All substance, energy, and life are the result of the Word of God being spoken, believed upon, and done. In Isaiah 48:3, God says He declared the former things from the beginning; they went forth from His mouth, and He caused them to be heard. Then suddenly He did them, and they came to pass. In the Genesis account of creation, we read how the Holy Spirit hovered over the face of the deep. Our Creator said, "Let there be light," and there was light. When we combine this account with 2 Corinthians 4:6,

39

we understand the command was for light to shine out of darkness. When God said light be, the Spirit hovering and waiting on the Word to be spoken did what the Word said. He became the essence of that Word spoken. Here we witness the cooperative faith of the Godhead in operation.

2. The Word provided operational order for the things we see and now know. The wisdom manifested in the intricacies of creation is the outcome of faith released by His Word.

3. The Word equipped this creation with purpose. Jesus said the words He spoke were spirit and life. Every function and role is masterfully employed by God performing His Word.

Hebrews 1:3 says He upholds all things by the Word of His Power. In 2 Peter 1:3, it tells us His Divine Power has given us all things that pertain to life and godliness. *When we combine these two thoughts from God's Word, we find the Word vested with His power giving us all things that have to do with our life in Christ and how we live in Him.* It is through faith we access this grace we are given privilege to stand in. It is through faith that grace is released and demonstrated by our lives into the earth, making the Kingdom of God known. Faith is the substance, the evidence of the things of God as they exist in the unseen realm.

THE DOOR OF FAITH

We learn in Genesis that God was forced to send Adam and Eve out of the garden because of the tree of life. A cherub was stationed to place a flaming sword that flashed back and forth to guard the ways of this tree. This remained in place until the tree was removed. If Adam had been able to access the tree while being separated from God, it would have plunged all humanity into an eternal existence apart from the Father. In John's Gospel, we read that God remedied this by sending Jesus into the world that we might have life and have it more abundantly. He made the way available to us through faith. As we receive Jesus, we become a partaker of His divine nature, eternal life. Thus, it is accurate to say faith in God's Word is the door to a life of fellowship and communion with Christ. It is in this fellowship we realize our identity, purpose, and authority, which comes from Him.

God has given us the privilege to approach Him through faith, and Colossians 2:14 says He removed all of the obstacles and hindrances that previously prevented us from drawing close to Him. He accomplished this through the cross of Christ. While removing those obstacles, Jesus entered into God's inner sanctuary for us.

If we consider this with Hebrews 9:12, 24, we learn that He not only entered the holy place beyond the curtain but appeared there for us, securing our eternal redemption. When we add Hebrews 10:19, we discover the promise that we can boldly enter heaven's Most Holy Place because of the blood of Jesus. The Apostle Paul writes in Ephesians 3:12 as translated in the NLT: "Because of Christ and our faith in him, we can now come boldly and confidently into God's presence." So our faith in Christ is our door to fellowship with our Father.

God's greatest desire is to bring many sons into His glory. The use of the words *sons* and *glory* in Hebrews 2:10 utilizes the idea of us being His glorious offspring through Christ. We are not only partakers of the divine nature; we are expressions of His Being. These scriptures we have just noticed describe the invitation and entrance God has provided unto us to come into His Presence. It is an awesome privilege to have the right to absorb these scriptures into our thinking so the power of God's redeeming grace can pour into our lives. As we come to an understanding of these truths, faith becomes the door granting us the right of passage and entrance into the inner sanctums of God's heavenly temple and glory.

As faith is our door, it is also our method of drawing near to God. We are promised that if we draw near to

Him, He will draw near to us. Hebrews 10:22 exhorts us to go right into the presence of God with a sincere heart fully trusting Him. The highest use of our faith is to earnestly believe God's Word to fellowship with Him in His Presence. That is what we are promised, and that is what we can have.

It's important to grasp here the significance of the glory. While we often associate this term with manifestations of God's power, the greatest use of the term is found in association with His manifest presence. *His glory is a direct result of an interconnected fellowship communing in the desire of the Father.* Throughout the Bible we find reference and association with worshipping God and the revealing of His glory. The Spirit of Christ is in us, crying out, "Abba Father!" Because of this, there is a passionate desire driving us to commune with our glorious Father. God has made a way into His presence available to us through faith where our rights and relationship of sonship can be fully realized.

We are instructed in Romans 13:14 to put on or clothe ourselves with the presence of the Lord Jesus Christ. To clothe ourselves places the responsibility of living in His presence solely upon us. It is through faith we access, draw near, and clothe ourselves with Christ Jesus, the express image of His Glory. We accomplish this through a confession of God's Word and a commitment to delighting ourselves in Christ.

There are many scriptures declaring and describing our relationship with God through His Son. We possess these privileges of sonship as we come to the place of believing we receive what we say. In Mark 11:23, Jesus said that if we "do not doubt in our heart but believe the things we say will come to pass, we shall have what we say." We must spend time meditating in these spiritual facts concerning our identity so we can experience the fruit of this awesome relationship God means for us to know because He has freely with Him (Christ) given us all things. While Adam could no longer access the tree of life, the thing I want us to realize is that the promises of His divine nature and presence are readily available to us.

The door of faith is a two-way door. *While it is the way we draw near to God and know Him, it is also the way He moves through us into the earth.* Throughout this book, we mention the Lord's Prayer. In this prayer, Jesus reveals God's original plan for the interaction between His Kingdom and the earth. Jesus told us that the Kingdom of Heaven was to come into the realm controlled by worldly influences.

We might draw the picture from this instruction that God was looking to invade a hostile territory and begin colonizing it. Jesus goes on telling us to pray that God's will be done on earth as it is in heaven. As we study this prayer, we discover God's agenda of working through us to restore His Kingdom environment and purpose in this world.

When we believe God's Word and carry out His instructions as revealed to us, God's Kingdom purpose is flowing through us. He is manifesting Himself upon our faith as it is expressed within His calling upon our lives. He desires to place each of us within a segment of society so that the earth and all that is in it is filled with His glory. That placement may be in the marketplace as an entrepreneur or business executive or anything in between. That placement may be in a traditional ministry setting within a church, or you could be someone sent to another country or culture.

The point I want to make is that each of us in the Body of Christ have a functional significance within the time we are given here on earth, and the anointing of God is to flow through us. As the purpose of God is established within our sphere of influence, waves of His love and power are to flood the world around us. Jesus said that if we could believe, we would see the glory of God. The Bible also says that His glory covers the earth as the waters cover the seabed and that the earth is to be filled with knowledge of His glory.

When we put these passages together, we learn that the awesome glory of God is ready to flow through our faith into the earth so that all who see may come to the knowledge of Jesus Christ as their personal Lord and Savior. God doesn't want to share His throne with other belief systems; He wants all people to experience His love and be free from the bondage of sin, fear, guilt, sickness, poverty, and grief. The Lordship of Jesus Christ is to be known by and through us.

THREE KINDS OF FAITH

The Bible speaks of three kinds of faith, and each administration of faith testifies of Jesus. He is Alpha and Omega, the Beginning and the End. All things are created by Him and for Him. He is before all things, and by Him all things consist. *As the source of all things, faith comes from Him and will testify of Him, declare Him, reveal Him, and manifest Him.*

THE MEASURE OF FAITH

The administration of the measure of faith speaks of gifting and ability. Paul tells us that a measure of faith is given to each of us. Just as our bodies have many parts and each part has a special function, so it is with Christ's body. We are many parts of one body, and we all belong to each other. In his grace, God has given us different gifts for doing certain things well.

God gave us grace and purpose in Christ Jesus before time began. This grace and purpose has provided us ability and gifting to fulfill His will. We see in Matthew's gospel an example of this in the parable of the talents. We find in the parable that the master's money was distributed to each of the servants in proportion to their abilities.

Their ability determined the value of the silver given to them. As the parable goes, two of the three put the investment to work. They experienced increase, which doubled the original amount given to them. So it is safe to say that their ability or gifting contained the potential to increase the resources their master entrusted to them. God has built this into every one of us. If something we are doing is not experiencing increase, we may not be in the right place, or we may not be fully managing our gifts and talents. All of us need to be sure we are not in fear as the one steward was found to be.

Since this is an illustration of the Kingdom of Heaven, I believe it is accurate to determine that the measure of faith given to us is empowered with a hundredfold anointing to increase that which we are given stewardship over. It is important to say here that they were able to manage what they were entrusted with. It is my experience that increase doesn't come from our ability alone but also from management of that ability. Remember, I stated the observation that each one's ability possessed the potential of increase. The effectiveness of our ability will rise to the level of our management capabilities. That's the reason Jesus stated that there were three increments of increase: thirtyfold, sixtyfold, and a hundredfold.

FAITH WHICH COMES

The second administration is described as faith that comes by hearing the Word of God. This kind of faith does not refer to our ability and gifting. It refers to the substance of the unseen realm. This faith must be developed through meditating on the Word of God. We find this in Romans 10:17 (NKJV) and Joshua 1:8 (AMP).

> So then faith comes by hearing, and hearing by the word of God. This Book of the Law shall not depart out of your mouth, but you shall meditate on it day and night, that you may observe and do according to all that is written in it. For then you shall make your way prosperous, and then you shall deal wisely and have good success.

We may be able to understand Romans 10:17 a little better said this way: faith comes into our heart through our ears as we continually hear what the Word of God says. God told Joshua that the prosperity of his way and the success of his ventures would come only as he was able to have an inward insight to the teachings and writings God gave Moses. This inward insight would enable him to possess the culture and behaviors of the Kingdom of God. In turn, this inward insight would lead them into the inheritance promised.

Jesus told the disciples on a certain occasion they had little faith. *The characteristic of little faith is believing what you see instead of what you say.* He also commended the centurion on his great faith. *The characteristic at this end of the range is believing what you say instead of what you see.* This range implies that there are degrees of faith, and this faith can increase from little to great. Paul bragged about the Thessalonian Church that their faith had grown exceedingly.

The people gathered around Jesus to hear Him and be healed of their diseases. They came to Him from all over the region. Upon the conclusion of Jesus' teaching, they were moved to do something they had not done. Luke 6:19 says, "The whole multitude sought to touch Him, for power went out from Him and healed them all." For them to seek to touch His garment, He must have given them direction to do so. He must have told them that if they would believe in what He said, they would experience who He is, and healing would flow from Him to them.

What they heard brought them faith to engage His power and receive the result of what He declared. Luke records that all were healed.

During the years of my ministry, I have witnessed thousands of people healed through the power of God. Yet very few of those healings occurred because of a miracle. Most of them happened through the preaching and teaching of God's Word. Most of them came to a point of faith to receive what the Word says, and God ministered to them through their faith.

GIFT OF SPECIAL FAITH

The third administration of faith is that which is called special faith in 1 Corinthians 12:9. This kind of faith differs from the other two as it is manifested in the life of the believer as the Spirit decides. It is often accompanied by the gift listed as working of miracles and can be experienced along with the one known as gifts of healings. This faith identifies a quality of superior ability, which transcends our thinking and reasoning faculties. When this kind of faith is in operation, we experience a confidence and boldness found in what we say and do. As a result, we realize the accomplishing of the miraculous. I recall an occurrence of this action of faith in my ministry. I had given an altar call for people who needed healing to come forward for prayer. I intended to pray the prayer of faith with them as I usually did. A man and his wife came forward, presenting themselves for hands to be laid upon them. I could tell they were unfamiliar with this practice of ministry and found out later they had never been in a service like this before. She began telling some of our ministry team about her husband's condition. He was being considered for a heart transplant because the majority of his heart no longer functioned.

To complicate this condition, he had a tumor in his colon the size of a grapefruit, and she was willing to provide medical documents to support their situation. As she finished speaking, something heavenly happened to me, which was totally unexpected. A wave of absolute faith and awareness of God's living power became evident within me. This was a manifestation of special faith. My reaction to this unexpected work of the Holy Spirit was with great authority and understanding. I spoke to him in an unassuming tone, commanding his heart to live. I also spoke to the cancer in his body and demanded it to die and be removed from his body. He smiled and thanked me for the prayer and returned to his seat.

If we were to look at things with the natural eye, nothing had changed. However, I believed God's Word, which said if I would declare anything in His name that He would do it. I remained in faith, although I didn't know the outcome of things from a medical point of view.

A number of weeks later, they stood in front of our church, testifying what God had done for him. He was no longer being considered for a heart transplant because his heart was operating at 100 percent and was as healthy as any young man. The oncologist treating his cancerous tumor was astounded at this man's condition, declaring that his tumor was completely gone and God had performed a miracle. This man traveled to many churches after his healing, giving his testimony of how God saved him and gave him new life.

We find Peter operating under this kind of faith in Acts 3. In verse 16, Peter talks about a faith that is through Jesus that made the man whole. This kind of faith is not a result of hearing the preaching and teaching of God's Word. Smith Wigglesworth describes the gift of special faith as an ability to speak a command beyond our personal ability. Dr. Lester Sumrall writes of Brother Wigglesworth:

> One day, when he came home from work, he was met at the door with news that his wife had died and that she had been dead for two hours. To that, Wigglesworth replied, "No, she is not

dead." He dropped his lunch bucket and tools, walked into the bedroom, pulled her out of bed, stood her against the wall, called her by her first name, and said, "I command you to come to me now!" Then he backed off, and here she came! She lived a number of years after that.

DYNAMICS OF FAITH

As mentioned before, Romans 10:17 tells us that faith comes into our hearts through our ears as we continually hear the Gospel of the Kingdom. The Word of God is the Gospel and proclaims the New Covenant written in His blood. His Word reveals His will and contains the power of promise to assure His faithfulness. The Bible says He could swear by none greater, so He swore upon His own self-existence that what He has said, He will do it. Jesus stands as our guarantee of this as He mediates our rights to be the recipient of the promises of God.

The word translated *hearing* in this verse refers to the literal sense of hearing, which can occur both on a sensory level as well as spiritual. In fact, scripture supports both levels are interdependent and are vital to the development, sustaining, and application of our faith. The sensory level begins the inner working of the spiritual. For faith to come, you are going to have to hear with your physical ear before you perceive with your spiritual ear. This word is commonly used in a continual tense of the verb, and we find that to be the case in its use in this passage of scripture.

The literal translation as I have stated gives the idea of continual hearing. This indicates the action of layering. We often think because we have heard something before, we understand the entirety of the content. We may have understood as much as we could at that stage of our spiritual development. However, this verb suggests we need to continually hear so that we experience a building up of our perception of Jesus and confidence of who He is. Often as we enter stages of spiritual development, the truth we thought we fully understood becomes fresh to us because a layer is being added.

This is what Paul meant when he said in Philippians 3 that he had not arrived or achieved perfection (full maturity [Ephesians 4:11–13, NLT]), but he pressed on to possess that perfection (full maturity). We will never in this life fully possess the stage where we cannot grow or advance in the knowledge of Christ anymore. There are continual layers being added as we advance in the knowledge and calling of God. When we reach the stage of development where our course is finished and our race is run, we will pass from this life to be with Christ, which Paul says is far better. So the continual hearing of the Word of God brings us to greater dynamics of faith and increase to our spiritual capacity.

It is accurate to say that as our faith grows, so does the dwelling place of Christ in our heart. Our perception (discernment) of Him grows as well. There are primarily three ways we hear the Word of God so that faith comes into our heart. Hearing the preaching of the Word of God as in Acts 14:7–10, hearing the Word of God taught as in Luke 6:17–19, and hearing ourselves meditate upon the Word of God as talked about in Joshua 1:8.

As we develop our confidence of trusting God, we also position ourselves for a greater measure of the power of God to flow into our lives. In fact, the stage of development we are living in determines the level of resurrection power flowing to us and through us. I have come to understand Ephesians 1:19 to say, "That we may come to the knowledge, discernment and comprehension of His exceeding great and mighty power which flows to us and through us who are believing."

This is illustrated in the ministry of Jesus as people responded to His teaching so they could receive healing and deliverance. In Mark 5:25–34, we read about a woman who had an issue of blood for twelve years. She had spent all that she had on physicians and grew worse with time. Then she heard of Jesus. She must have heard the teaching Jesus taught to the multitudes in Luke 6:17–19. He must have taught them that He came from God and that He was anointed to heal the sick. He must have taught them that this anointing to heal whatever sickness or disease they had was tangible and transferable to His clothing. He must have taught them that if they would believe what He said and in who He is, all they had to do was touch His clothing and that anointing would flow from Him to them.

The Bible says they sought to touch Him, and all of them received healing and deliverance for their lives. She believed what she heard because Matthew's gospel says she said within her heart, "If I can touch His garment, I will be made whole." In her statement of faith, there is no questioning of His will to heal her. Her healing is a finished fact as far as she is concerned. Her greatest challenge was her need to get close enough to touch His garment. Because of her condition, it was probable she would be refused public access. So she came behind the crowd and maneuvered her way to the back of Jesus.

From there she anonymously reached out and touched His garment. At that moment, healing power left Jesus and went into her. In verse 34, Jesus says for her to go her way, her faith has made her whole. This is direct testimony that faith in Jesus' words brings confidence to receive from His anointing. Everyone who can believe can receive from the power of God.

Section 2

FAITH WITHOUT WORKS IS DEAD

FAITH WORKS FOR US

The concept of faith working may be a new perspective for some of us. However, I believe that as we discuss this concept, we'll find that this is the way God cares for us. The scripture exhorts us to cast our care upon the Lord. This is terrific in theory, but how do we really do this and refrain from getting back into worry and anxiety over the situation? Our faith is His agency for getting the things He wants for us to have into our lives.

The Bible is filled with examples of how people turned things over to God and trusted His faithfulness. Such an example is the story of Jehoshaphat, who chose to believe the prophetic word in spite of the evidence. Another is the courage of ten lepers who were told by Jesus to go and show themselves to the priest. They were challenged to deny the apparent symptoms evident in their bodies while believing their cleansing would manifest by the time they arrived at the priest's house. All ten men experienced healing as they traveled because they turned their sickness over to His Word while counting Him faithful to keep His promise.

Sometimes this means we have to trust Him beyond the apparent outcome and believe that He is caring for us in a bigger picture than we are able to see at the moment.

Another example of this is found in John 11 with the story of Lazarus, Martha, and Mary. The crowning statement of Jesus in John 11:42 is "Did I not tell you that you would see the glory of God if you believed?" Jesus told the crowd in Mark 9:23, "All things are possible to him who believes." If we combine these two statements about our faith, we will discover the seed of possibility and glory is in our believing. I remember something Brother Hagin would always say: "Just keep the switch of faith turned on." This is what Jesus said to Jairus in Mark 5 when He told him to fear not the report of his daughter's death, only believe.

Hebrews 11:1 in the Bible says, "Now faith is the substance of things hoped for, the evidence of things not seen." I often ask people, as this is so, what are you hoping for? It seems our hope is the measuring cup of our faith. There is a difference as well as a contrast between the Bible word *hope* and the word commonly used in our vocabulary. Our use of the word *wish* corresponds with the word we normally use for hope. It carries the idea of what we would prefer to see happen, but the outcome is according to an array of possibilities. In essence, it is much like predicting a hurricane's behavior. We hope the storm doesn't affect our lives, but we really don't know the outcome of the forecast.

The Bible word for *hope* means "to expect with confidence and anticipation." This indicates an expression of our preference and desire mixed with a fully persuaded expectation. This expectation is completed in the work of Jesus Christ as we understand it. Ephesians 3:10–11 states that God's eternal purpose for everyone who believes was accomplished in Christ. This removes the possibility of variables because all of what God is going to do has already been done. All which has been accomplished is reserved for us to enter into through faith in God's Word. This is the message of good news, which is Christ in us, the Hope of Glory.

The Biblical word *hope* as used in Hebrews 11:1 relates to faith in that it is where you dream and release your confidence in the possibilities of God. Our hope is not based on what we see in the natural realm, but what we see in God's Word. Paul refers to Abraham and how that against hope (what was expected because of the evidence), he believed in hope (what he expected from what he saw in God's Word). Abraham was very aware of his circumstances as they appeared naturally. Yet he chose not to consider the personal inability of his own body or the barrenness of Sarah's womb. He fixed his eyes on the imagery of God's Word.

There are events that happen to us that bring us across a certain maturity threshold where our life is never the same. One such event happened to me during my first international ministry trip in 1994. I received an invitation to speak to a group of Christian ministers and leaders in the country of Belarus. The four-day conference was held in a large auditorium in the capital city of Minsk. God did many great things for the people there, but what He did for me was during the return trip. I had booked my travel itinerary through a reputable travel agent, and because of my schedule, I arranged to depart from Minsk on a day in which there were no international trips scheduled. I didn't think anything about travelling domestically in this part of the world, but I didn't ask many questions either. It turns out that I flew into Moscow to catch an international flight back home. The travel agent didn't think I needed a Russian visa since I was only passing through the airport for a connecting flight. That was not the case.

Upon leaving Minsk, I caught a flight into a domestic airport, which was abandoned and derelict. Much of what I'm about to tell you I found out later from a friend who lived in the area.

It was one of those times where ignorance was bliss. Upon arrival, I left the aircraft and stumbled past the people who were living in the structure. After walking around a bit trying to find my luggage and the connecting flight information, I walked into the middle of an underground gambling operation. Once I realized my situation, I became overwhelmed with fear. The only thing I knew to do was get somewhere and start praying. I found a place in the room filled with people who had been transported in for gambling and began praying in the Spirit. After a short while, I sensed the fear melting away, and once again my confidence and trust in God rose up to take over my thinking.

At that moment, I said aloud, "Lord, you told me to come here, so I know you are going to get me home. I need you to send me someone to help me who speaks English. Thank you for favor in Jesus' name." I had just finished getting those words out of my mouth when a well-dressed man whom I had not noticed before came walking toward me. Now you have to understand my dilemma. There I stood, a non-Russian–speaking person, trying to find my way around in a place renowned for unlawful activity. From all appearance, I was at a great disadvantage and was vulnerable.

This man speaking kindly to me asked if I needed direction. I explained to him my situation, and he inquired as to what kind of currency I was carrying. I told him I was carrying US dollars. Though I knew it was dangerous to be telling him this, I trusted God, believing that the angels who were with me were greater in number and power than the forces assigned to destroy me. He helped me to obtain a taxi to the international airport for $25. The airport was just over one hour away, and it was quite a trip. I was told that I should have paid $250 for that taxi ride.

When I arrived at the international airport, my troubles really surfaced. I was nearly arrested twice for not having a visa. As I was being interrogated, I tried to tell them I was just passing through to go to the United States. The customs and immigration people didn't believe me because I had travelled domestically into Russia. The officer questioning me was a Russian military officer, and he became very frustrated, saying, "For the last time, what are you doing in Russia?" After answering this same question a number of times, I replied, "I am a preacher of the gospel of Jesus Christ. Do you believe in Him?"

His posture changed along with his facial expressions. He looked at me and then toward the door, releasing me to catch my flight. Just as I was about to enter the gate to board the plane, I was taken into custody again and interrogated. This time I was being questioned by a different officer, and she was not considerate of my story. Just when it looked as if I was going to be removed from the airport by military personnel, a telephone call came through to the chief officer who had been questioning me. When she returned from the phone call, she said to me, "You are free to go!" I boarded my flight, which was held up for three hours, and early the next morning, I made it home exhilarated while exhausted.

The reason I have shared this story is because throughout this ordeal, the thought never crossed my mind that I would not make it home. My hope was steadfast. I fully expected God to work things out to get me to JFK for my connecting flight to North Carolina.

This was the hope Abraham experienced as he believed in an outcome beyond the apparent circumstances governing his situation. God continues to demonstrate faithfulness to His Word.

Another word synonymous with hope is *desire*, and it is used in connection with faith in Mark 11:24 where Jesus said, "What things so ever you desire, when you pray, believe that you receive them, and you shall have them." Notice He said that we should believe that we receive them.

The reference of "them" is talking about our desires or hopes. This is what marks our praying and receiving from God. The desires that make up our portfolio of prayer can't come from our connection to the necessities we are aware of. Our dependence and trust in God that is related only to our needs often relates more to what we don't have in our possession as opposed to what we do. It causes us to see the glass half-empty instead of half-full while identifying an underlying fear that these needs are not going to be met.

When Jesus' disciples were faced with a seemingly impossible task of feeding a crowd of many thousands, Jesus asked them to perform an inventory check of what they had. The point I want to make is that our needs are not met because we are lacking. Our needs are met because we have been a good steward of the things we have. As with the account of the disciples feeding the multitude, the little they had became more than enough when seasoned by the multiplication anointing of Jesus. *The seed for their need was always in their possession.* It is the same with us as well. Our desires come from the hope manifested in our heart.

It is apparent that everything God has committed to us is seeded into our lives through our hope. He has given us all things richly to enjoy. He has deposited our complete inheritance into the Word of God, which places possession into our authority. As far as God is concerned, everything we are to receive from Him is past tense. When Jesus cried from the cross, "It is finished," He proclaimed that all of God's blessing and grace has just been released because of His blood sacrifice for all humanity.

Everything possible has already been supplied and released for our possession. Again I want to reference

Mark 11:24, which says, "Whatever things you desire (hope for confidently expecting to receive), when you pray, believe you will receive them, and you will have them." This verse again places significant emphasis upon our need to believe so that we may possess the things God has reserved for us.

Our hope is where the glory of God in Christ is planted. When we spend time ministering to the Lord through worship, prayer, and meditating in God's Word, we come into contact with His desires for us. He says the thoughts and plans He means for our lives are for good and not for disaster, to give us a future and a hope. This would indicate that God's eternal purpose along with our identity is deposited into our hearts through the hope given to us. In Romans 15:13, it is declared that we should abound in hope by the power of the Holy Spirit.

Previously in my ministry, I can see where I have not placed enough emphasis upon the subject of hope. The eternal expectation of God in His glory lives in our hearts according to Colossians 1:27. When our hopes are what God plants into our hearts, there is a vision and reality of that Word, which becomes fuel and identity for our faith. That is when faith becomes the substance of things hoped for, the evidence of things never before seen.

RELEASING OUR FAITH

For faith to become substance, it must be released. Most of us have lived long enough to experience more than our share of struggles. We have come to realize deliverance doesn't come just because we believe it should. Those of us who have stumbled into this presumption recognized God's ability and thought that was sufficient. We just knew somehow God would work it out, only to be horribly disappointed and sometimes disillusioned. James teaches us that it's not enough to just believe because faith without works is dead. The Apostle Peter adds that demons believe and tremble as well. For our salvation to be fully realized in our life, it requires more than just believing in God's ability to do for us what we need for Him to.

Again we look into the gospels to find someone Jesus said was in faith who received the desire of their heart from Him. Oftentimes we find ourselves in a debate as to how to believe God for answers to prayers and for miracles. The people who received from Jesus in His day are just like we are in our day. We can learn the pattern of faith from them. If it worked for them, it will work for us. In regard to how God works in our lives, there is no reference to then and now. Jesus is the same yesterday, today, and forever. God does not react with us according to preference. Using the woman's story of receiving healing from an incurable condition as an illustration, I want to point out four markers that describe the biblical pattern of believing God and receiving what He has for us.

THE FIRST MARKER BEGINS WITH WHAT WE HEAR

The woman with an issue of blood heard the words Jesus taught, and these words gave her hope for wholeness. God will utilize a variety of communication media to get His truth into our hearts and minds. Often the first question is not "What do you believe?" but "What and who are you listening to?" Solomon tells us in Proverbs 4 that his father, David, urged him to set his mind on what he told him. As scripture, God is urging us to give attention to His Word. He has placed spiritual voices into our lives to hear from as well. To what and whom we are giving our attention to is of utmost importance as we follow Christ.

This woman got her mind off the fact she had been sick for twelve years. She quit thinking about the fact she had emptied her bank account seeking medical treatment, and she stopped focusing on the fact there was nothing the doctors could do for her. She chose to consider Jesus and give attention to the words she heard about Him. The Bible says we must give attention, listening very closely to the Word we have heard unless we drift away from its significance and meaning in our lives.

THE SECOND MARKER IS OUR ACTION

As we consider this woman acting upon what she heard, we find her saying something. Our faith speaks and acts as a seed. From what we read of this account in Matthew 9:21, she apparently spent time speaking to her situation before she approached Jesus. Some people would think she had more problems than an incurable blood disease because she was talking to herself. She was practicing something Jesus spoke about on several occasions, and that is speaking to your mountain to be removed from one place to another. This disease was her mountain.

This example teaches us that we often have to spend ample time speaking what we believe to ourselves until the substance and confidence of faith rises from our hearts to dominate our thinking. It is then we become persuaded of the truth of God's Word, allowing it to rule our situation. The Bible says that what we think of ourselves determines our perception and the enemy has spent a great deal of time and energy influencing our thinking and perception. For the culture of the Word of God to become our first nature, our thinking that shapes our perceptions must be changed. If we will take the time to renew our minds with our confession of faith, we will change our perception and experience a manifestation of God's salvation.

The scripture in Romans 10:10 says that "with our heart we believe unto righteousness and with our mouth we confess our salvation." *When we look at Mark 11:23, we discover Jesus focused three times more on what we say in comparison to what we believe.* The Apostle Paul quoted scripture from the book of Psalms when he declared, "We believe and also speak." There are numerous scriptures throughout the Bible that places primary emphasis on what is said from faith. Our believing is released through our speaking. The confession of our mouth manifests our salvation through Christ. This woman said, "If I may touch his clothes, I shall be healed."

If we connect this thought with Ephesians 2:8, which says, "For by grace you have been saved through faith," we find that we enter into God's grace and power with our confession of faith. Remember, Paul said that Christ dwells in our hearts through our faith and that the exceeding great power of God flows toward us who believe. In Abraham's encounter with God in Genesis 15, his confession was childlessness, and that is what he possessed. After his time with God, his confession changed to "So shall my seed be," and that is what happened.

We are each and every one an expression of God's express purpose and will. God has hammered out the details of our life of victory and salvation through the work of Christ on the Cross. God said through Isaiah by the Spirit that He works from the end to the beginning. When the scripture says we are the wisdom of God, He is saying that He has filled our life with His purpose, power, and victory. God says in Ephesians that it is through us He has chosen to display His multifaceted wisdom. Our lives are on display before the angelic rulers and authorities for their instruction. Thus, God has established the order of command to come through our faith. As we speak what we believe, all the agencies of heaven go into motion to accomplish the mind of Christ and enforce what has been accomplished through and by Him.

THE THIRD MARKER IS POSITIONING

She had to maneuver herself into position to touch his clothes. Many people don't understand the necessity of positioning themselves. One common factor we find connected to almost everyone who received from Jesus' ministry is that they positioned themselves. I'm reminded of the Syrophenecian woman who came to Jesus petitioning for her daughter's deliverance. Because she was a Gentile and not a Jew, her access to Jesus was restrained. The Bible said she kept crying after Him as they walked along the road, so much so that the disciples wanted Him to grant her petition and send her away. Yet Jesus continued to ignore her. Finally she positioned herself in worship, facing Him. Jesus could not turn her away, and she received what she came for. Jesus said to her, "Woman, great is your faith. Your petition is granted."

The woman with the blood disease we are focusing on could not position herself in front of Jesus; however, she did what it took to get into His audience. It is possible we can sit in front of our television and receive what we are praying for. That may be the best we can do at the moment. However, this method of exposure and audience cannot become a convenience for us. Often we have to go beyond what is convenient and easy in order to release our faith and receive from what God has intended for us.

The woman learned of this message of Jesus from someone who had been present at the event reported in Luke 6:17–19. Each of them in this passage who were suffering got up from where they were and came to be in His audience. Some of them traveled from a great distance paying a great price. Every one of them who touched His garment was healed. They paid a price for their positioning, as did this woman who was plagued with a blood disease. She too experienced healing for that which doctors could not treat.

THE FOURTH MARKER IS A TESTIMONY OF PRAISE

Notice the woman with the incurable disease not only confessed her faith that her healing would occur, but she fell down before Jesus and told him everything. Jesus told her to go her way; her faith had made her whole. We can combine this with the healing of the Samaritan leper in the seventeenth chapter of Luke's gospel. He returned and gave Jesus a testimony of praise with thanksgiving. Jesus said the same thing He did to the woman: "Arise, go your way. Your faith has made you whole." Their testimony declared the finished work of their faith. Their praise went before their wholeness.

Early in my pastoral ministry, I became connected to a family who had two beautiful children. The youngest was born autistic, and this child was very difficult to manage. I prayed with the family on several occasions as we talked about the possibilities of faith in God's Word. At this time the child was four years old and becoming very violent and destructive. The parents had come to their last wits' end, and the doctors were telling them there was little they could do other than to place him in a controlled environment. This was unacceptable as the parents had come to a place of believing God for their son's healing. The mother would regularly testify to the congregation the she knew Jesus was going to heal her son.

Upon the close of a Sunday morning service, the mother brought the child to me for prayer once again. I felt her frustration, and after praying for her, I told her that I would call upon her to bring him forward when I perceived it was the timing from God to pray for him. She was very disappointed, but she stayed in confidence that the Lord was going to heal and help her family.

After a few weeks on a particular Sunday, I had scheduled a guest speaker to minister to our church, and at the close of his time of ministering, I stood in front of the congregation to bless them and send them away. It was at that time the Spirit of God moved upon me to call for this mother and her son to come forward. When I did, she leaped from her seat, dragging this child with her to the front of the church. You had to have been there to capture the scene I am trying to explain to you. He was kicking and screaming and trying to get loose from her grip. I think the power of God was as much upon her to control him as He was upon me to pray for him.

At that moment, the spiritual force dominating this child fully manifested. I spoke to the spirit manipulating this child's mind and commanded it to leave while placing my hand on him, speaking healing to his body. He immediately became quiet and passive while falling to his knees. The overwhelmed mother sank to hers as well as I asked the child to look at me. As he did, I touched his mouth, commanding his tongue to be loosened. You see, up to this point, the child had not spoken clearly and it was almost impossible to understand what he was saying. As soon I removed my fingers from his lips, he looked at his mother and told her he loved her and that Jesus healed him. God healed that child right there and then. Twenty years later, I attended his ordination service as he entered into the ministry to become a pastor himself.

From that Sunday morning until now, that mother never misses an opportunity to share her testimony of praise concerning her son. As I watched this family over the next several years, I am convinced that her and her son's praise sealed his wholeness and ushered him into the life he has today.

GOD WILL NOT BE PUT IN A BOX

The Bible in its entirety is the whole expression of Jesus. Yet it is the Holy Spirit who guides us into its application for our lives. For instance, we have the promise we may receive concerning divine healing, even as Israel had during the days of Jesus' ministry. We also know from the gospels that the healing power of Jesus was available to all who could or would believe. However, we see Jesus' ministering healing in a number of different ways. The same thing applies in our lives of faith and prayer. The Holy Spirit may lead us to have hands laid upon us so we may receive healing. It may be we can pray the prayer of faith and receive without anyone's involvement. Yet the next time we need to apply the healing provision to our lives by faith, the Holy Spirit may instruct us to contact someone we are in relationship with to pray with us the prayer of agreement.

There are times we need medical doctors. While all things are possible to him who believes, there are

DANIEL EPLEY

occasions where God uses doctors and medicine to accomplish His blessing and will. I remember one certain occasion where a brother in the Lord was in need of a miraculous healing. He had experienced many healings and miracles in his lifetime and was strong in faith for this one.

Yet it was apparent that God was working in him concerning releasing control and trusting Him. God arranged through a series of miraculous interventions of favor for this brother to receive the medical and surgical treatment he needed. His recovery was so miraculous it testified to everyone on the hospital floor of God's power. If we attempt to apply God's provision of grace to our lives as we see fit, we often are disappointed. God will not be put into a box. Every time we yield to the Holy Spirit's leading, we will experience the fullness of victory and peace.

Sometimes we don't receive what we believe in because our priorities get out of balance. I recall an incident in my life where I was in need of healing from a viral respiratory infection. I had lived in divine health for twenty-five years without a symptom of any kind. Up to that point, I had lived by my confession of faith concerning healing in my body.

Because of a very hectic schedule, I allowed my time with the Lord to start slipping away. I had continued to pray and meditate upon His Word, but I wasn't spending the kind of time in His Presence I was accustomed to. As I referred to this before from the book of Hebrews, we need to continually give attention to the truth we have heard unless we begin to drift away

78

from it. Without my realizing what was happening, I was drifting away from the truth. The confidence I had experienced for my life was becoming stale and brittle.

This respiratory infection did not respond to my words as I commanded it to leave my body. It became necessary for me to seek medical attention, and they did all they could do. I became like the woman in the fifth chapter of Mark with the issue of blood disease. I was spending all I had and was not getting better. Months passed by, and three doctors, two specialty clinics, and three x-rays later, I wasn't improved.

During this time I continued to travel and minister to people all over the world. While I was praying for the sick and witnessing profound miracles in other people, I became amused that I was physically worse off than most of the people I was ministering to. After five months of this dreadful condition, it became apparent that I needed to seek God on this and discover His wisdom of how to apply His Word as my healer. It was then I realized how I had drifted away from the confidence of His Word I had walked in for so many years.

I took some time away from my schedule and shut myself up to minister to the Lord and seek His face. I don't know why it took me so long to do this. Day after day for one week, I became stronger and stronger spiritually as I lay before the Lord. I declared a fast into the second week and spent time meditating in the Word concerning healing truths. I continued to get stronger; however, the symptoms persisted. One day while ministering to the Lord, I perceived His voice speaking to me that I had allowed my priorities to become all mixed up.

Sometimes we seek God for wisdom, but when we hear from Him, we are not ready to listen to what He has to say. He showed me how I had become out of balance in seeking Him in prayer for what I could do for Him. It was painful to realize I had lost my first love in that I had ceased to seek Him out and fellowship with Him for who He is. My personal times with Him had become seeking moments for the anointing to serve, not for the anointing to progressively become more deeply and intimately conscious of Him. I've got to tell you, I was heartbroken. After I wept and repented, I adjusted my perspective and rediscovered my first love.

It was there I began to experience the authority I had lost. On May 20, exactly six months to the day I had become sick, I spoke to these symptoms in my body with a renewed confidence and authority. I slept through the night for the first time since I had become sick, and the next morning I awoke in perfect health and strength as if nothing had ever happened. Hallelujah!

Each day is that which He has made, and our steps are ordered for breakthrough, hope, joy, and victory in that day. We understand in Proverbs 4:23 that out of our inner being flows the boundaries of our life. As we allow the mind of Christ by the Word of God to permeate our being and become our culture, we display the good, acceptable, and perfect will of God. We also know from Luke 6:45 that Jesus said, "Out of the abundance of our heart our mouth speaks." As our mouth speaks from the abundance of peace and truth in our heart, we enter the perfect will of God for our lives.

There is a saying that our confession rules us. I like to say our confession makes us because we believe in the God who brings life to dead things and declares those things that do not exist as though they did. He is our pattern, and we are told to possess and exhibit His faith, imitating His ways. Speaking our faith is how we partake of the provision of the Kingdom of God, and this provision is contained in the Word of His grace. There are several occasions in the Epistles the Apostle Paul exhorts the reader to "put on" or be clothed upon with the things of God. This metaphor illustrates the believer's role in partaking of the divine nature that God has made available by and through what we.

HOW GOD RESPONDS TO FAITH

There are three things about God that we should realize when we discuss faith. As we realize these things, we'll discover that what God does for us is His best. God responds to faith because it is the way He reacts to Himself. Throughout Jesus' ministry, we find Him walking out His faith relationship with the Father. One statement Jesus made revealing His frustration was "How long shall I put up with your unbelief?" God reacts to faith because faith is the operative action of the cooperative Godhead.

FIRST THINGS FIRST

First, God responds to faith because faith engages His purpose and good pleasure. This is expressed through His Word. For God's purpose to be accomplished, this expression of His Word must enter into the spirit of man. Faith carries out God's express purpose for

His good pleasure and glory. God is alert and active, watching over His Word, ready to perform it for it will not return unto Him annulled.

In reading John 16:13–15, we hear Jesus explaining how His power moves from Him to us. He reveals to us that it is the Holy Spirit who delivers the substance of His Lordship into our lives and sphere of influence. What is it that moves Jesus to make these things known unto us? It is evident that as we meditate upon the Word of God, the Spirit is guiding us into all truth. Upon His guidance, we are putting demands upon Jesus. He goes to work within us to publish God's good pleasure. As we draw near to Him, He draws near to us. He is waiting on us to press upon Him with His Word. He is ready to pour through us the substance of the Father. This is how He has chosen to make His name known, evoking change to people and circumstances around us.

A personal example of this happened in my life as I went to minister in England. It was my second trip of ministry to this particular area, and I was very excited to follow up on the tremendous move of God's Spirit we all enjoyed upon my first trip. As I prayed seeking God for the trip, my mind was conditioning this time of prayer with the thoughts of duplicating the results experienced during the previous trip.

While in prayer, the Lord impressed upon me He wanted to manifest a healing anointing throughout the region where I was ministering. The city is made up of six towns, and I was preaching in four of the six. I was honored to be invited to minister in several churches, and everywhere I went there were phenomenal miracles and healings. The last day of my visit I attended a minister's prayer service in which several different denominations from all of the six towns were present. As we closed out the prayer session, I was asked to speak to the ministers. I asked them to reflect upon the previous two weeks and testify of how the Lord had moved in their churches and ministries.

Each of them began to tell of wonderful occasions of healing and miracles that had just broke out in their services. Many of these dear pastors were shepherds of denominational churches who didn't regularly experience this kind of thing. Pastors, chaplains, and school principals all testified of astounding healings that occurred in their places of Christian service. One pastor spoke of an instance during his sermon about a woman who stood up in the middle of the congregation and began shouting, "It is gone! The pain is gone!" The startled pastor stopped his sermon and asked the woman what was wrong. She reported that she was diagnosed with cancer and was experiencing severe pain in her body. In an instant, the pain was gone, and the tumors that were apparent had disappeared. The next several minutes were spent in thunderous praise unlike that church had ever experienced.

As we all rejoiced while we heard such powerful testimonies, I asked them as to when they began to notice the healing manifestations. They all said the healings began about two weeks before. Later I realized a parallel to the timing of my arrival and after discussing

it with my host Pastor Phil Parsons, we both rejoiced
and gave glory to the Lord.

GOD DOES NOT HAVE FAVORITES

Second, as God responds to faith, He does not have
any personal favorites. God's blessing does not follow
the path of favoritism to its destination. God did not
bless Abraham because He personally liked Abraham
above other people. God's act of blessing Abraham
was in response to Abraham's obedience. Abraham
obeyed God by believing in His Word. This enabled
him to enter into what God had prepared for him. This
provided a path for God's blessing to flow to Abraham.
I have heard it said that faith moves God. I agree
with that to a degree, but I would rather say that faith
engages God.

*God's plan to use people to deliver His desire into
the earth is noted throughout the Bible.* His method of
delivery is through covenant relationship. This is seen in
Genesis 15 as God entered into covenant with Abram,
promising that He would bring his children to the land
of promise.

God has entered into covenant with us through
Christ. Within this covenant, He has given us great
promises or pledges. The main point of this covenant
is God has placed upon us the responsibility of the
first move. This is a great picture of His overwhelming
love for us. He has placed all of who He is into these
promises and made Himself accessible to us through
faith.

Thus, James exhorts us to draw near to God, and He will draw near to us. It would seem that God is waiting on our action so He may react. As we look deeper into this subject, we find it is God who begins the action of our heart with a cry of "Abba Father." So He is initiating the inclination of our first move for us, but it is our responsibility to react and yield to His leading. So we can conclude that He is generating the action of our drawing near to Him so He may react to us.

The greatest example of this is found in Genesis 22. God calls on Abraham to sacrifice his only son at a certain place on a certain mountain. Notice the scripture passage in verse 2 records God as referring to Isaac as Abraham's only son and the son whom he loves. It is no accident or coincidence that God uses the same phraseology describing His son in John 3:16.

Abraham knows he has received his son by and through faith. He also knows his son is the fulfillment of God's promise to him as it was spoken, "If you can discern the multitude and galleries of stellar constellations, so shall your seed be." He also knows God told him that "in Isaac shall your descendants come forth." So as Abraham responds to God's call upon him to sacrifice Isaac, he knows that whatever happens, he and his son will be returning home.

As the story goes, Abraham drew back his knife to fulfill the command of God, and a ram was available for the sacrifice. Here's one of the things to see here: God called upon Abraham to do something through faith, which would engage God to do the same thing at a later time. Abraham's obedience engaged God's purpose, plan, and power to be manifested in the earth. God mirrored Abraham's action by sending His only son, the son of His love to be sacrificed for the world's sin.

THE WORD IS GOD

Thirdly, God responds to faith in His Word with power because He and His Word are one. He has magnified His Word above His name. The statement "God is faithful" accurately describes God's nature of reaction. That means God has bound Himself to doing what He says. This is His nature and the only way He can react. When we respond to His Word, which includes our trust in His character, God moves according to that response. Let's take a look at the scripture in Matthew 14:23 where Peter and Jesus walk together on stormy waters. Peter calls out to Jesus to identify himself with the word *come*.

Peter's confidence in Jesus and His spoken word is graphically portrayed. That confidence is the result of His relationship. Peter knew that if the person he saw walking on the water was Jesus, the word He would speak would come from the power sustaining Him upon the water. That word from Jesus would contain that same power enabling him to do the same thing Jesus was doing.

I find inspiration that Peter believed he could do anything Jesus did as long as he had a word from Him. The remarkable fact that Peter went out of the boat illustrates Peter's overwhelming confidence in the person of Jesus. His action also reveals the integrity of God's Word as it identifies the power available to all who will believe.

FOUR STEPS OF ABRAHAM'S FAITH

In Romans 4:12–25 from the Message Bible, we read about the steps of faith that Abraham had. Paul implied that these are our steps as well. I have identified these four steps as they apply to our lives of faith, enabling us to walk out the salvation of God even as Abraham did. In another place, the Apostle Paul tells us that we walk by faith and not by natural sight. It also is evident that we have spiritual eyes as well as natural ones from which we can see the things of God. It is then my conclusion that we walk where we see God's Word, and this is the walk of faith. These four steps are what we do about our mind and our thinking when we are in the midst of believing for the miraculous, even while we are surrounded by the riptides of unbelief.

THE FIRST STEP OF FAITH

The first step of faith is a personal decision to go God's way. In this decision, there isn't any room for double-mindedness. This first step sets the stage for all the other steps to follow. It talks about our attitude. The Bible tells us in Hebrews 11:8 that Abraham's journey of faith began with obedience. He set his life in order when he chose to obey God's direction. It is clear throughout the scriptures that our life and purpose have been predetermined and predisposed by God. And as great as that sounds, it is also evident this truth does not overstep our decision to obey or disobey Him. We can choose to go God's way or our own way.

When Abraham believed God's Word, he then entered into the fullness of God's plan, which was fully put together for him. God had already worked out all the details and knew where every rough spot would be while weaving into the fabric of time a way of escape and salvation. Abraham's faith set God's eternal purpose in motion, engaging every agency heaven has to ensure the probable outcome. Read this key verse and notice that Abraham then entered God's purpose, provision, and miraculous power when he believed.

> That famous promise God gave Abraham—that he and his children would possess the earth— was not given because of something Abraham did or would do. It was based on God's decision to put everything together for him, which Abraham then entered when he believed."
>
> Romans 4:12 (MSG)

The word given to Israel by the Prophet Isaiah is also good for us who say, "If you will be willing and obedient, you will eat the good of the land." Therefore, our lives are made up of seasons in which we experience the great love of God appealing to us for a choice to obey Him. Each season is meant to mature us by preparing our decisions and actions for a display of God's wisdom.

Every season is defined by our personal maturity as it is demonstrated by our faith working through love. The call of God upon Abraham's life to separate himself from his father's house and come to an undisclosed location is definitely an illustration of God moving and positioning us for the fulfilling of His purpose. Abraham transitioned from one season to another by faith in the revelation of God's Word he received.

We can know when we are about to pass from one season to the next by the friction in our lives caused by obedience. Each one of us knows that every step of obedience is a step into an awesome life in Christ. Yet we also realize that each step is also a move away from the familiar and comfortable. In this we experience pain and death to the things of our past and of this world. Sometimes it involves changes in relationships. This is the friction caused by obedience. When the friction eases and we have come to a place of complete surrender and trust, we will find God working in our lives with increase, guidance, and blessing.

There are times we become frustrated because it seems the increase, guidance, and blessing are late. The truth is they are held up either because we haven't made the right choices where obedience is concerned, or we are still going through the test that makes up the end of the season we are in. Remember Joseph in Genesis 40, when after ten years of imprisonment, he thought he would be remembered for his ministry to Pharaoh's cup bearer. He remained there for two more years before it was time for his next season.

When his obedience was fulfilled, he experienced increase, guidance, and blessing. These three are the fruit of obedience, and they will launch us into our next season. Obeying God through faith was Abraham's first step, and it is ours as well.

THE SECOND STEP OF FAITH

The second step of faith is "When everything was hopeless, Abraham believed anyway, deciding to not live on the basis of what he saw he couldn't do but on what God said he would do." This step tells us that there are going to be times those things we believe for look impossible. And if we were to go by the evidence of things we see, we would never receive the evidence of things not seen. Abraham had to choose to believe in what God said about him and his life. His faith would influence how he saw things around him. Instead of seeing obstacles and impossibilities, he saw God's probabilities.

Often we are persuaded by the evidence we see and hear concerning the situation we are in. There is a popular saying I hear quoted a lot, which says, "It is what it is." While there is some truth to that, it is not an all-inclusive statement determining the final outcome. With a word from God, we see things differently.

I remember how God has worked in my life time and time again where I could have made decisions according to what was fact and reality. Yet burning in me was a creative truth that redirected me from the obvious direction and led me into blessing. Every time I have chosen to see things the way God sees them, there has always been an appearance and manifestation of the miraculous and the heavenly.

In August 2007, the Lord spoke to me about a door He was opening for me and that I should go through it. If I were to speak to you from a reasonable mind, it didn't look like there was any chance for these things to be a possibility. A big part of this was the element of relocating my family from our lifelong home surrounded by family and friends to a city where we would not know anybody. And oh, by the way, the expense of securing a home and moving was in need for a miracle as well. In the midst of these apparent obstacles, I held my ground because I believed I had heard a Word from God.

I found favor with that decision maker, and that door did open just as God said, and I walked through it into the blessing God had for me. We found a home perfect for us, and the finances needed for the move came in. And on a side note, I didn't advertise this or petition for support.

I know there are times in which God directs us to publish our needs, giving people an opportunity to sow and partner with our grace, but not this time. I sowed an offering toward the provision and spoke to it to come to me, believing I would possess what I said. God moved as He said He would, and we moved like He said we would. Many years ago, I heard it said, "I refuse to be influenced by what I see or hear, only by what I believe." I liked that and adopted this statement to be an anthem in my life.

THE THIRD STEP OF FAITH

The third step of faith is considering not your inability. This step has to do with our thought life. The book of Proverbs says, "As a man thinks in his heart, so is he." The greatest battle in the good fight of faith is in our thinking. Where our thinking stands on a subject or situation defines our position to receive from God. The scripture says in the book of James that a double-minded man is unstable in all of his ways, and this man should not think he is going to receive anything from God. The double mind will always wind up with the conclusion that is from unbelief. The renewed mind will wind up with the conclusion that is from God's mind. Let's look at how Abraham's thought processes defined his success and fulfillment.

> Abraham didn't focus on his own impotence and say, "It's hopeless. This hundred-year-old body could never father a child." Nor did he survey Sarah's decades of infertility and give up. He didn't tiptoe around God's promise asking cautiously skeptical questions. When everything was hopeless, Abraham believed anyway, deciding to live not on the basis of what he saw he couldn't do but on what God said he would do.
>
> Romans 4:19 (MSG)

According to this verse, Abraham focused on something besides himself. He didn't focus on what he couldn't do at the moment but on what God said he would do. Something must be done about what we are considering while what we believe in is coming to pass. If we are not going to consider the deadness of our situation and the report we have heard, we must consider something. The writer of Hebrews tells us we should consider Him who died for us and bore our curse, redeeming us from the deadness that the curse brings. Every time the evidence of those things shows up, we must say what the Word of God says in Jesus' name. We should remain consumed by the pledge of God like Abraham did as "he continually plunged himself into the promise and came up strong, ready for God."

THE FOURTH STEP OF FAITH

The fourth step of faith is being fully persuaded that God would make good on what He said. It's so easy to be persuaded of your circumstances. The fourth step has to do with our reasoning faculties. Our reasoning is the result of our mental and behavioral preparation to react. There are so many occasions where men and women have reacted and responded heroically to a situation, only to hear them say afterward they were acting upon their training. How they responded was an engaged reflex of their conditioning and preparation. This fourth step is about conditioning and preparation, which causes us to react with faith to a crisis or difficult situation.

There will always be that occasion where we must stand upon what we have already received from God's Word, even when there is no outward evidence of its reality. Socially and economically, Abraham had been blessed for His obedience to God's Word. The promise to Abraham that lingered was that of being made a nation. It is apparent that after the encounter with God in Genesis 15:1–6, Abraham would take a stroll in the evening, looking at the stars while rehearsing what God had said to him. He would do this for ten years before the promise God gave him would come to pass. This would prove to be his conditioning and preparation.

It is evident that the older he became, the younger his body became. As all natural strength and ability faded, faith in God's Word became the ascendant and superior factor in Abraham's condition. His confession of faith being "So shall my descendants be" called those things that did not previously exist into reality while causing the deadness in his body to experience life. The creative and healing force of God's Word will cause dead things to live, barren wombs to bear, blind eyes to see, deaf ears to hear, and the wonderful experience of becoming a new creation in Christ Jesus. Because of this phenomenon, Abraham lived another seventy-five years after the birth of Isaac, continuing to father children in his old age.

The main key to persuasion has to do with the choice to continually nurture what you believe and stand firm with your confession. Abraham became fully persuaded by giving attention to the things that He had heard. There is so much competition for your mind. To what you give attention to will determine the fruit of your walking by faith.

Section 3

FAITH WORKS THROUGH LOVE

LOVE IS

Throughout forty-plus years of Christian faith, I have found conclusively that love is the essence of the Godhead. His identity of love is how He expresses Himself. We also understand that love is the revelation declaring who He is. The Holy Spirit further exemplifies this truth to us as we find Jesus describing God as a Spirit in John 4:24 and again identifies God in 1 John 4:8 as love. If we combine these two descriptions of God, we learn that God is a Spirit of Love.

It has become my experience that this love is expressed to us through Jesus Christ. As He is referred to as God's Son throughout Scripture, we find He is also recognized as the Word. The gospel of John says, "In the beginning was the Word, and the Word was with God, and the Word was God. He was in the beginning with God." *Therefore, the Word describes and manifests God's great work of love toward us as well as in us.* I believe it is beyond our natural comprehension to fully grasp God's love for us because we are always measuring it to our relational experiences. As great or poor as they may be, nothing compares to the piercing purity of God's love and the warmth we experience from Him.

We also discover as we learn of God's love that it is not based on merit or debt. God's love is grace to us, and this grace is expressed through faith. The topic of grace also connects us back to the Word of God because faith comes by hearing the Word of His grace. Therefore, our faith works from this premise that it manifests the love of God. It would seem we have gone in a circle describing the connection between God's love and His Word. I have done this because it is vital to our growth and development that we understand this connection.

God gives us an example of this in Luke 2:52. This scripture tells us that Jesus increased in wisdom and favor with God and man. Notice in this verse that there is a distinction in the favor of God and the favor of man. The increase described here speaks of Jesus becoming more connected to His identity as the Word and His relationship with the Father. This relationship is a love relationship.

The more we grow in this connection, the more we experience increase in wisdom and favor with God and man. As God can trust us in love, He will bring us into greater spheres of influence or favor with men. It is this truth that determines the level of impact we have with the audience God has given us to reveal His love to. As ministers, we often judge our effectiveness by the scope of growth in the size of our ministry. The primary strategy and agenda to growing in ministry influence and effectiveness is to grow in love while becoming more and more like Jesus.

As we have studied in previous chapters how faith works, we find in this chapter that faith works by love. So it is accurate to say that everywhere we read about faith working, we must include the subject of love. An example of this is in Ephesians 6:16, speaking of the shield of faith. This portion of the armor of God enables us to quench all the fiery darts of the wicked one. In this activity, if we disregard the truth about love, our faith shield will not work, and we will experience a barrage of fiery darts. The love of God not only manifests through our faith, but our faith also expresses itself through our love. Since love is such a powerful force of emotion, connection, and consciousness, let's look further into its meaning.

There are several Greek words for love, but we are going to focus on three. These words are frequently found in modern as well as ancient Greek texts. They are *eros*, *philia*, and *agape*.

EROS

Eros is passionate love, carrying with it the sense of desire and longing. From this word comes the Modern Greek version *erotas*, which means erotic or romantic love. The term *erotic* is most identified with sexual expression; however, *eros* does not have to be sexual in nature. *Eros* can be interpreted as a love for someone, which is beyond the friendship love described by the word *philia*. This love describes the expression and connection between two people united in their emotion as one soul. We find this kind of love between David and Jonathan. Though their relationship was not sexual, it was stronger than that of friendship. The Word tells us David and Jonathan were knit together as one soul.

I believe our passion for the Word of God is a great a contributor to our comprehension of spiritual truth. In comparison, it is equally as significant as our understanding of the Word. The psalmist David in Psalms 42:1 sang, "As the deer longs for streams of water, so I long for you, O God." *Our passion for the Word of God exhibits our desire to go deeper with Him.* To go deeper, we must experience an increase of depth in ourselves. The scripture talks about the depths of God calling out to the depths of man. Our passion represents that dredging process of removing all the silt and sediment that have worked its way into our lives. As God increases our passion, we begin to dig deeper into Him, and He starts digging deeper into us.

It is a behavioral fact that we are all driven and defined by our passion. This is best illustrated by the woman who ministered to the Lord in the book of Luke 7. Jesus said she loved him much, and as a result, she was moved to extravagant worship and adoration of the Lord.

PHILIA

The word *philia* is found in ancient Greek manuscripts often written as *phileo*. This form of the word is found in the New Testament eleven times. It is used to describe the relationship of friends and the strong connection of affection without the sense of erotic passion. The contextual use of this word in scripture often describes a strong personal bond with someone or something, such as Jesus with Lazarus in John 11:3, 36 and Peter's response to Jesus in John 21:15–17.

AGAPE

The word *agape* is the most common-used word for love in the New Testament. Along with its Greek sibling *agapao*, it is found 260 times referring to a range of descriptions of love. It is used in contextual settings as a verb and a noun. This word means love as it is understood in the bond of relationship and self-sacrifice. It carries with it the characteristic of faithfulness. This love will not deny us, hurt us, or leave us while believing the best of us. Agape describes the covenant bond between two people or groups and gives us insight into the very nature of God.

Paul tells us in Romans that the Holy Spirit is given unto us, and He pours into our hearts the love of God. As we have discussed, this love is a revealer of God's nature and person. As we identify with Christ, we have to recognize that if God is a Spirit of love, then so are we. We are created in Christ's image and likeness. So the great passage of love in 1 Corinthians 13:4–7 describes us as well as God. Because of our shared identity, we can substitute our name where a reference to love is. We can speak this about our self while believing we are who we say we are through faith.

FAITH WORKS THROUGH LOVE

We need to continually meditate in this text to renew our mind and to define our life and behaviors. Jesus said the world would know us by our love for one another. This word should never depart from our lips as we speak it concerning our lives as well as others for whom we are praying. I have personally experienced great renewal in my life because of this as well as seeing others changed by the Spirit of God as I prayed these verses over them.

As we have discussed how faith works through love, we all must realize that our faith is going to grow and increase as our consciousness of love grows and increases. This truth is also evident concerning the Presence of God and the anointing. In the midst of Paul's prayer for the church as written in Ephesians 3:18, he prayed that Christ, who is the anointed one, and the anointing would dwell in the believer's heart through faith. This is not referring to being born again but pointing out that the indwelling reality of Christ in our lives is a growing and increasing experience proportioned to our faith in His Word.

There is a principle found in the Bible that governs the operation of faith manifesting the things of God. This principle is found in Galatians 5:6, saying, "Faith works through love." For us to experience an increase of the presence and manifest anointing of Christ in our lives and ministries, we must grow up in the realities concerning our relationship with Him through love.

THE LOVE CULTURE OF CHRIST CONTROLS US

Our life as it is now is a composite of patterns established in our thinking. This makes up our culture. I heard a statement a few years ago that started an evaluation of my approach to embracing change: "Nothing changes until something changes." While that sounds simple, it implies that our cultural patterns will continue to determine our outcome until we are exposed to a different perception of thinking. I witnessed this level of change in my daughter's life. She was in her last year of college and living at home at the time. God directed us to move to a city sixty miles away from our lifelong home. She had always lived there; her friends, relationships, and family were there. She could have remained; however, she believed she was to move with us.

This move produced a change of environmental exposure for her that resulted in a radical redirecting of her spiritual life. This became the foundation from which her thought processes changed and resulted in decisions altering the course for her life. She graduated college with honors and began to fulfill some of her lifelong dreams, traveling across the United States and ministering in churches with a worship ministry group. She soon realized her call from God into ministry and experienced an opportunity to go on staff as a worship leader and ministry director for the youth department at a church in the city we live in. I am convinced that if she hadn't made the move with us, she would not be involved with ministry as she is now.

Jesus took this precept to the next level when He said in Matthew 6:31, "Therefore do not worry and be anxious saying, what are we going to have to eat; or what are we going to have to drink; or what are we going to have to wear?" *Jesus is telling us that when we speak the thoughts going through our mind, we are giving a place for them to take up residence in our thinking.* Once a thought has residence, it becomes an opinion, which, in a short time, becomes a belief. So Jesus is teaching us our authority over what we think and believe.

Thoughts originate from several sources, including the unseen influences of angels and demons. Therefore, we can take a thought or cast it down. This act of authority is done through speaking. This is what Paul was talking about in 2 Corinthians 10:4–6 when he wrote about pulling down strongholds while casting down imaginations and every obstacle of pride and fear. These things gain a foothold, positioning themselves against our minds and attempting to block us from knowing God. As we are casting these things down, we are bringing every thought into captivity, forcing it to submit to the revelation of Christ we hold dear.

This is the importance of renewing our mind in God's Word. In Romans 12:2, Paul tells us, "Do not be conformed to this world, but be transformed by the renewing of your mind, so that you may prove what the will of God is, that which is good and acceptable and perfect."

This scripture is the New Testament counterpart to what God told Joshua: "This book of the law shall not depart from your mouth, but you shall meditate on it day and night, so that you may be careful to do according to all that is written in it; for then you will make your way prosperous, and then you will have success."

To meditate is to speak to yourself repeatedly while thinking and exploring the truth you are meditating on. The Spirit of God transforms us through this mind renewal process, proving in our lives the good, acceptable, and perfect will of God. Our composite patterns change, so our life changes; prosperity and success start manifesting as our behavior patterns become aligned with His Word. This applies to developing our minds and lives in a love culture.

Everything about us is a product of the streams of thought we allow to flow through our minds. That which occupies our thoughts will translate into our speech, either silently or verbally. As said before, the more we speak of a thought brings it to an opinion, and the more we incubate an opinion brings it to an influence of belief. The scripture in Proverbs that says "As a man thinks in his heart, so is he" is a core truth to our development as a person, community, or a population at large. The influence we yield to as truth affects the life flow, which comes out of our heart. Proverbs 4:23 tells us, "Watch over your heart with all diligence, for from it flows the springs of life." Jesus said in Luke 6:45 as it is translated in the New American Standard Bible, "The good man out of the good treasure of his heart brings forth what is good; and the evil man out of the evil treasure brings forth what is evil; for his mouth speaks from that which fills his heart."

From the combining of these two scriptures, we can determine the boundaries evident in our life are the result of the knowledge present in our heart. This knowledge becomes the substance of our lives along with the behaviors that govern us as it is conveyed by our words.

This is the point I want to make about a love culture; the Apostle Paul exhorts us that our lives are to be controlled by the love of Christ, which pushes or compels us to continue behaving through love. This compelling influences us to consider Christ and His gift of life to all, not the deadness and corruption that rules our flesh. The love of Christ causes us to consider everyone according to His redemptive work of taking our place for the judgment of sin. The prophet said in Isaiah 53:6, "We have all gone astray as wayward sheep, each of us turning to our own understanding and ways; and the Lord has laid our iniquity upon Him."

It is very easy for us to take into account the faults and shortcomings of someone's fleshly actions, yet Paul said that he didn't consider anyone after the flesh. *One of the characteristics of God's love poured into our heart is that love believes the best of every person.*

When we recognize people by the sacrificial death of Christ for them, we take into account God's hope and potential as it is resident within their lives. We provide an atmosphere of faith, believing that their actions and behaviors can change. By considering other people in this way, we create and sustain an environment for their redemption, deliverance, and growth into spiritual maturity.

I can recall a number of people whose personality and behaviors could really get to me. One in particular was a man I worked with who was not a Christian and had a difficult attitude and mannerism. As his supervisor, I wanted to make things as difficult for him as he made them for me. I began to develop a wrong attitude to the point I couldn't stand the guy. One day on my way home for lunch, he was in traffic ahead of me, and the thought went through my mind of just how much I disliked him. I then shook my head to clear out that thought and began to pray. I confessed to God, who knows my heart and thoughts anyway, that I had the wrong attitude and needed His help to love this man. As soon as this request left my heart and before it could completely leave my lips, God poured upon me a love for him that was incredible. Sitting there in traffic with tears rushing down my face, I considered him differently. Instead of holding disdain for him, I loved him. I began to look for ways to bless him and show him Christ. His attitude and actions no longer got to me because I considered him differently.

My life changed drastically when this happened. My attitude toward him also began to affect how he behaved. His behavior and mind-sets began to mirror how I was treating him, and he became quite a success as his life began to change. Before I resigned that position and accepted a full-time ministry invitation, he and I had become friends, and he would listen to me about Jesus' and God's great gift of peace and love for us.

His change of attitude happened because I exercised the love of God toward him, and he experienced that love instead of the rejection and judgment he had become so familiar with. This must be how Jesus ministered to the prostitute. Her transformation from a woman who had committed many sins to a woman expressing extravagant worship did not happen because of the judgment and rejection she had experienced from the religious leaders of that day. It happened because of the love Jesus expressed toward her as he considered her according to the hope and potential God had for her.

The life-changing anointing of the Holy Spirit for our lives as well as our ministries is a love exchange. Jesus saved, healed, and set free the multitudes because He loved them. The miracles we experience from God are not because we deserve them; it is because He first loved us. *The word compassion describes a divine release of faith through love, which carries the yoke, destroying anointing.*

During my journey of Christian ministry, which began in 1982, every instance of any release of God's life-changing grace has been an exercise of compassion.

Many times as I have witnessed the greatness of God's intervention in people's lives, I have wept because I experienced the compassion God has for them. The development of our love affects every aspect of our Christian life, especially our ministry.

THE REST OF LOVE

There are many religions in the world who claim to have a relationship with God. At the core of their belief system is a "performance" paradigm, which positions each participant under a need to do the actions required for acknowledgement and achievement. This pattern locks them into a life of underachieving, frustration, and condemnation. It is the latter point that alienates them from true fulfillment.

In Christianity, the relationship with God is through faith in His son, Jesus Christ. The one defining point at the core of this belief system is that Jesus comes to dwell within every believer, and every believer dwells in Him. This difference positions every believer inside a "know and believe" paradigm instead of a model whose focus is on performance.

This locks every believer into freedom because Jesus took care of our condemnation. *As a man, Jesus took the sin of humanity and satisfied the requirements God expected of us where performance is concerned.* This truth places the inheritance God gave to Jesus available to everyone who will believe. That inheritance includes righteousness, favor, and a life in fellowship with the Father. It declares us free from condemnation while granting us ascendancy and dominion over spiritual death, sickness, poverty, and everything else that has a name.

The Apostle John considered this inheritance as an endowment of love. As children of God, we have been given the privilege of coming to our Father without reservation or fear. Our privilege of access is a core benefit of this endowment. Our Father loves us so much that He has made us favorable, holy, and without fault in His eyes through Christ. This assures us of our access to Him.

This is the truth God wants us to absorb and know because it is the criteria for dwelling in His presence. We don't possess holiness and guiltlessness because of what we have done. We possess these things because of faith in Christ. None of us live sinless lives from a performance perspective, yet we have forgiveness granted to us because of faith in Christ's blood. When we confess our sins to him with the attitude of repentance, we experience the forgiveness and cleansing from all unrighteousness He has earned for us. This is what the Apostle John calls perfect love.

God not only wants us to absorb this truth, He wants this truth to be our lifestyle. Guilt will reduce our ability to know and experience His Presence. Our Father cannot fellowship with guilt and condemnation. He has provided this perfect love that removes all restraint and apprehension preventing us from drawing near to Him and experiencing His precious Person.

We understand from 1 John 4:18 that fear has an expectation of punishment and, with this, administers torment. The rest of love given to us is a life free from fear of punishment, a life of boldness and confidence in our faith. Again I want to mention this love has been bestowed upon us, and we engage this love through our attitude of repentance from sin and confession of our faults to Him. While God does not want us in sin, He does not want us in guilt and fear of reprisal either. God wants us to be fully mature, living in the rest of His love while knowing the great grace and mercy He has expressed toward us.

THE WISDOM OF LOVE

The scripture in Philippians 1:9–10 is another one of the New Testament prayers Paul prayed for the churches. I believe all scripture is inspired by the Holy Spirit, so I believe this is a Word from God for us today. I am persuaded it is important for us to know and experience the revelation and power God has for us here, so I want to extract certain content and explore the relevance of this scriptural prayer.

> And this I pray: that your love may abound yet more and more and extend to its fullest development in knowledge and all keen insight [that your love may display itself in greater depth of acquaintance and more comprehensive discernment], So that you may surely learn to sense what is vital, and approve and prize what is excellent and of real value [recognizing the highest and the best, and distinguishing the moral differences], and that you may be untainted and pure and unerring and blameless [so that with hearts sincere and certain and

unsullied, you may approach] the day of Christ
[not stumbling nor causing others to stumble].

Philippians 1:9–10 (AMP)

THAT YOUR LOVE MAY ABOUND YET MORE AND MORE

The Spirit of God through the Apostle Paul reveals to us that we have the capacity to grow, increase, and abound in love. Actually, the use of the term "more and more" indicates a progressive expansion of our ability to know and experience God. As we have already learned, our faith capacity as well as our anointing to serve is tethered to our development and growth in love.

In examining the truth of verse 9, we find there are measures and levels that are applicable to our relationship with God. This is identified in the phrase from the scripture "That your love may abound yet more and more and extend to its fullest development in knowledge." So we discover in this reference that there is a fullness to our development. This fullness is recognized in our depth of acquaintance with Christ and the increasing of our comprehensive discernment. So as our love abounds more and more, so does our relationship with God. While knowledge involves knowing the particulars about a subject, it's also about experiencing. Peter replied to Jesus, "We have believed and have come to know that you are the Holy One of God." The use of this word *know* includes the action of experience in addition to believing. Now we can lay hold of the truth of our focus verse; as we develop and grow in the love of God, we also increase in the knowledge of Him concerning all wisdom and spiritual understanding.

SO THAT YOU MAY LEARN TO SENSE WHAT IS VITAL (RECOGNIZING THE HIGHEST AND BEST AND DISTINGUISHING THE MORAL DIFFERENCES)

I heard Dr. Mike Murdock say, "Wisdom is the skill of knowing the difference." I want to draw our attention to the first part of this sentence, which says, "Love enables us to sense what is vital." Let's look at the word *sense* because this word leads us into thinking about our perception. Apostle Ron Carpenter says that we receive things and people on how we perceive them. With this understanding, our ministry gift is received how others perceive us. The wisdom of God's love enables us to perceive clearly and accurately. There were many times in Jesus' ministry that it seemed He knew what people were thinking or saying privately to one another because of His perception. The Apostle Paul perceived the importance of conferring with the apostles in Jerusalem about his ministry. As we develop our heart and mind in love, we are sharpening our spiritual perception tools.

Jesus told us it was not for us to know the times and seasons God has put into His authority. Yet we can perceive and detect when a seasonal shift or change is coming to us. Love is the womb from which everything from God passes from Him to us. It is the governing factor to the wisdom of seasonal shifts and changes that occur in our lives. In the book of Galatians 4:1–2, we are introduced to the wisdom of God's love concerning maturity.

One of the ways to read and understand this scripture is to realize God's wisdom of revealing Himself to us according to the seasons of life we live through. When we combine the language and analogy of maturing from childhood to manhood with 1 Corinthians 13:11, we find some great similarities.

"When I was a child, I used to speak like a child, think like a child, reason like a child. When I became a man, I did away with childish things." Notice the three areas identifying the growth stages of our life. They are speaking, thinking, and reasoning. These three behavioral actions determine our maturity and readiness for the next season of God's grace for us.

He is at work in us both to will and do his good pleasure. It is our responsibility to put on love and yield to His working in us. Much of what we are waiting on God for is connected to our commitment to live in love. The guardians and managers mentioned in this scripture are people, situations, and circumstances that are meant to help us accomplish this development. As we mature in love through what we say, think, and reason, we come to the place and time (season) appointed by the Father for a portion of our inheritance to be manifested to us.

AND THAT YOU MAY BE UNTAINTED AND PURE AND UNERRING AND BLAMELESS

It is through the wisdom of love we live a life of character, displaying the person of Jesus Christ. As hard as we may try to be perfect, we all fall short of that goal. The wisdom of love shapes our thinking and habits, molding our behaviors so our lives can be faultless. Our testimony and example of faith is to be the blueprint for those who follow us as well as those God has given to us so we can bring them to a deeper knowledge of Him. The tragedy is there are no occasions of stumbling in the faith that is secret. Someone is always going to be affected by our foolishness.

We learn in Romans 8:13 that we overcome the ruling effects of our flesh by and through our life lived in the Holy Spirit. Throughout the New Testament we are instructed to put off the works of the flesh and in some cases put them to death. These works war against the knowledge of God in our lives. Many people have great struggles with these things as they endeavor to walk with God. The continual presence of sin in our minds and actions will result in a mindset grounded in condemnation instead of freedom and liberty. God does not want us living every day feeling filthy, defeated, and unworthy of His great love. He has provided a great promise of redemption for all of us through faith in the blood of Jesus. Paul tells us that we are to cleanse ourselves from all filthiness of the flesh and the spirit. This begins with changing our mindset concerning guilt and condemnation while choosing to partake of the inheritance of forgiveness, righteousness and freedom. The habits and impulses which often control us can be neutralized and rendered defeated as we exercise faith in His Word and drink from the supply of the Spirit given to us.

As we reflect upon these verses in Philippians, let's go back to the first four words, which are "And this I pray." *The increase and growth we have discussed is obtainable through prayer and specifically by ministering to the Lord by the Spirit*. Praying in the Spirit is a method of drinking from the presence of God. Jesus said, "If any man thirst, let him come to me and drink." There must be an act of drinking from Jesus that brings us to a point of overflow, which pours out of us. The analogy of flowing rivers is used by the Lord in the passage found in John 7. The flowing rivers, which He explained described the Holy Spirit and Jesus, said He had not been given to them yet. So there would be a time that this manifestation of the Spirit would be evident and available.

Since the result of drinking from Jesus is being full of the Holy Spirit, the analogy He is using implies that we are drinking from the Holy Spirit as we come to Him. In another passage found in Ephesians 5, Paul exhorted us not to be filled with wine but to be filled with the Spirit by speaking. When we splice these references together—from Philippians 1, John 7, and Ephesians 5—we discover that we experience an increase of the Holy Spirit as we pray by the Spirit. In other words, as we spend time praying in other tongues as the Spirit gives us utterance, we are drinking from

Jesus, and He is causing us to increase and come to an experience of overflow, which describes the living waters He is talking about in John 7.

As we explore the subject of prayer and being filled with the Spirit, we can also look into the connection between prayer and being filled with the wisdom and understanding of God. Paul is praying a New Testament prayer for the Ephesian Church and asks God that they would be filled with the Spirit of wisdom and revelation in the knowledge about Him. As we are filled with the Spirit and increased by Him, we also abound in love with greater measures. This is an awesome truth about prayer; it is a powerful force at work within us as well as through us. God is at work in us to know the wisdom of love so His glory will be manifested through us.

Section 4

FAITH AND THE FLOW OF THE ANOINTING

THE ENVIRONMENT OF FAITH

When we talk about the environment of faith, we are speaking about a spiritual climate favorable for God to occupy our lives. This spiritual climate provides the surroundings suitable for the habitation of God. In the beginning, God created such an environment so He and Adam could fellowship. This environment was an extension of the heavenly connecting to the earthly. It is evident that the heavenly and earthly were so closely aligned that God and Adam could pass from one to the other. The law of faith was a constant because fear and unbelief didn't exist.

What many have failed to understand is that God placed the lordship of this environment into Adam's care. In fact, we find the responsibility to sustain and implement that spiritual environment always being in man's authority. A climate is defined as the pattern of atmospheric conditions as it applies to the environment of a particular location. *Thus, an environment is the sum total of all the natural components as they exist while sustaining their purpose in the environment.* Prolonged change occurring in the contribution of any of these components will result in an environmental change. As it is in the natural, so it is in the spiritual.

Upon Adam's sin, the spiritual climate he had enjoyed was changed. This change resulted in Adam's inability to remain in the garden, which meant he had to be removed. The fact that Adam died spiritually meant that he would experience a reduction in the measure of the Presence of God, thus affecting the spiritual environment. It would be several hundred years later that this dynamic would be manifested in man's body, resulting in physical death. This environmental change was also witnessed in the moral decay of man's resolve and knowledge of God. This would mean Adam had to be removed from the place God made for him. From that point forward, he would have to use his authority to create such an environment for fellowship with God.

Just a side note, the core element that caused separation of the two realms was man's disobedience. So it is man's agreement with God resulting in obedience that brings the two realms back together. This applies the authority God has entrusted to us concerning the spiritual climate and environment. Before the redeeming work of Christ in the earth, God made Himself available through prayer and sacrificial offerings. Each sacrificial offering found in the Old Testament is a type of Christ. This being understood, our life of prayer and faith in Christ applies the obedience that God responds to. It is here we create, sustain, and implement the spiritual environment necessary for the abiding presence of God. It is up to us to draw near to Him through faith.

We find throughout the Bible that God has revealed and manifested himself by measure to man. In the beginning, it is evident that the fullness of God walked the earth with Adam in full measure. After Adam's sin, the measure began to reduce because of the corporate effect of man's fallen nature. John the Baptist testified of Jesus that He had the Spirit of God in full measure; however, each believer experiences a partial measure. This measure can be increased or decreased. When we come together in an environment of faith, we experience fellowship with God in a much greater measure.

Each one of us is a steward of the grace of God given to us. As we are found faithful to our stewardship, we each experience a greater measure of His grace. Our stewardship is judged through our agreement with God's Word and obedience to the leadership of the Holy Spirit. When we contribute this measure to a corporate setting, such as a local church body, we bring the element of fullness that has been entrusted to us.

This is the reason we need to realize the importance of being connected to the place and people God has connected us to. Paul said in 1 Corinthians 12:18 that God has set each member in the body just as He desired. Notice it is not as we desire or decide appropriate or advantageous. It is as He wants. Each one of us brings a supply of the Spirit of Christ, which contributes to the overall growth of the body and the building up of the environment in love.

It is to this end I call it an environment of faith because it is not made of things seen or existing but of the attitudes that are unseen. There is something worthwhile to be said about colors, lighting, and sound. All of these empower the human soul to demonstrate the innermost portions of our expression. Yet I have seen God sweep into a place without all of these wonderful props and move mightily, declaring His awesome Name with wonders beyond my comprehension. The unseen values determine the spiritual environment and atmosphere conducive for a glory storm.

It is the divine exchange, which occurs during our encounters with God, that invests, develops, and characterizes these unseen values. We commune with God through His Word as well as by the Spirit. As we delight ourselves in Him during our communion, we experience this exchange. It is this exchange that God provides for us that is effective in the development of an atmosphere conducive for His presence. The Apostle Paul declared to the Corinthian Church that God was his sufficiency.

I want to illustrate this with the story of Enoch walking in fellowship with God. He was walking in the same sufficiency that Paul referred to. Adam would have been 557 years old when Enoch began to walk with God. Adam could have taught him what he knew because Enoch discovered the environment of faith. Enoch might have learned from him the sensitivity needed to walk with God in that measure of His presence. Through utilizing what he possibly learned from Adam, He accessed the door of communion and fellowship. He walked with God by faith for three hundred years, and God removed him from the earth.

It's interesting that Adam was alive for all of Enoch's life. It could be suggested that the earthly spiritual climate became less and less favorable for the habitation of God. Enoch had experienced God in such a measure that God removed him from this world because the climate was not suitable to sustain that level of fellowship. God removed the door, taking Enoch with it. It has become my experience that once we have enjoyed and become cultured to the Presence of God, nothing else will do. The scripture says Enoch was removed so that he would not see death. God removed him so that he would not have to suffer the removal of the measure of fellowship and communion he and God was accustomed to.

> By faith Enoch was taken up so that he would not see death; AND HE WAS NOT FOUND BECAUSE GOD TOOK HIM UP; for he obtained the witness that before his being taken up he was pleasing to God.
>
> Hebrews 11:5 (NASB)

This door has been restored for us through Jesus Christ. Jesus said that He is the way, the truth, and the life, and no man comes to the Father except through Him. This truth is related to us again in the book of Ephesians telling us that we have access unto the Father by the Spirit through Christ. The book of Hebrews explains that we have access into the Holiest (of Holies) through the blood of Christ and that He as

131

our forerunner has entered into this place for us. As our forerunner, He has restored through His blood the way into the Presence of God and for the Presence of God to come to us.

There have been shades and shadows of this level of fellowship over the years, but I anticipate God wants to invade the earthly environment once again with that level of His glorious presence. *We need to discover our authority of providing a corporate environment suitable for the habitation of God so He can enter the earth as He desires in these last days.*

God has given to us the responsibility to create this environment by producing the spiritual climate necessary. On behalf of the unsaved and those who haven't grown into the benefit of spiritual authority, it is certainly up to us to provide the climate and environment for them to know God. There are four truths I want to share with you concerning creating a climate and environment of faith.

FIRST TRUTH IS PRAYER

In Matthew 6, Jesus taught us to pray, and He instructs us to declare the will of God to be done in the earth as it is in heaven. By instructing us in this way, He places this interrelation of heaven and earth into our authority. The emphasis here is not petition but the declaration of our faith as we understand our identification with Christ. In this we take our place of dominion through Him as kings in the earth. There is nothing in the scriptural text of this prayer suggesting we pray with petition concerning this. Yet there is all evidence suggesting we call for the Kingdom to come. As we pray and declare God's Word, we create the suitable climate. So Jesus gave us this model, saying, "Pray, then, in this way: 'Our Father who is in heaven, Hallowed be your name.' Your kingdom come your will be done, on earth as it is in heaven."

There is the time to intercede and petition God. The Apostle Paul wrote to the church in the book of Ephesians that we should pray at all times in the Spirit by utilizing all manner of prayer and petitions with supplications. Prayer, petitions, intercessions, supplications, and declarations all create an environment of faith because they require faith to engage God. It is through and by prayer we draw near to God, and He draws near to us.

When we survey the Old Testament concerning the times when God manifested Himself to Israel, these times were mostly centered on the sacrifices called for by God. Each of these sacrifices was a type of prayer and proclamation. When the fire of God fell in Leviticus 9:22–24, there was the presence of prayer and sacrifices. When the fire of God fell in response to Elijah's challenge of the prophets of Baal in 1 Kings 18, there was prayer along with a burnt offering. On the day of Pentecost as the fire of God fell upon the Church in Acts 2, there was the action of continual prayer.

As we look further into the prayer life of Jesus, we learn important truths about how heaven and earth interrelate. While Jesus walked the earth as a man, He was anointed by the Holy Spirit and identified as the Holy One of God. In John 1, the scripture declares

Him to be God. Jesus tells us in John 14:12–14 that He is our pattern for everything, which He will do through us in the Kingdom as it relates to the earth. Jesus spent an incredible amount of time in prayer, often praying all night.

He demonstrated the absolute need to create, cultivate, and sustain an environment of faith and communion through prayer. We could think that the miracle of Lazarus's resurrection happened because Jesus is God, and He could do anything He preferred. However, we learn in John 11 that Jesus prayed and communed with the Father about that event. There are two powerful facts related to this act of prayer in the life of Jesus that are worth taking a look at.

The first is revealed in Jesus' prayer as recorded in verses 41–42. This reference concerning the Father hearing Him must be reflected by His statement in verse 4. Jesus declared that Lazarus's sickness would not result in death but would serve to the glory of God. Yet we know that Jesus said to them plainly in verse14 that Lazarus is dead. Jesus created the climate for Lazarus's resurrection through a prayerful declaration of His faith.

This brings us to the second powerful fact, which is that the tangible manifestation of the glory of God is contingent upon the atmosphere and environment of faith. Now it was important for Him to create a climate that would encompass Martha and Mary, providing a corporate environment. We know from the scripture His plan all along was to raise Lazarus from the dead, even after four days. Yet when He spoke to Martha in verses 23–27, He spoke to her about believing. Again in verse 40, He makes a remarkable statement concerning believing, saying if we would believe, we would see the glory of God.

SECOND TRUTH IS HONOR

The second truth I want us to look into is honoring the Lord Jesus and the ministry gifts He has placed in our lives. In Matthew 10:40–42 and John 13:20, we read that if we receive and honor the one He has sent to us, we receive and honor Him and the Father who sent Him. As we receive and honor the ones He has sent, we create a climate and environment of faith. Jesus said in doing so, we will experience faith's reward, and the greatest element of that reward is the Presence of Jesus Himself.

As we continue to look into the ministry of Jesus about the environment of faith, we find the effect of dishonor. Jesus called this unbelief in Mark 6:1–6 as stated in the Amplified Bible. We learn in this passage it was God's will to do great things during His ministry trip to Nazareth, which included mighty miracles and healings. We also see that their lack of faith in Him prevented His perfect will from being done. He even laid his hands on a few people with minor ailments and healed them, hoping to perhaps stimulate the people of Nazareth to believe in what they heard Him teaching. Here again we discover the importance of an environment of faith in connection with the manifestation of God's mighty power.

Another thing to discuss about honor is our respect and honor of the Holy Spirit. We should regard His presence with a worshipful and prayerful attitude. Paul warns us in Ephesians not to grieve the Holy Spirit. In another place, he calls it insulting the Spirit of Grace. There are many ways this is done; selfishness and arrogance are at the root of all of them. This pushes Him away, greatly reducing His ability to influence our lives with His love and glory. As we honor Him and give Him the place of preeminence He deserves, we enjoy waves of His manifest presence, which increase in measure as we learn to obey and cooperate with Him.

THE THIRD TRUTH IS AGREEMENT

The third truth I want to observe is an attitude of faith and agreement. I have found over the years that my life has been enriched with people who just choose to believe. I have also encountered those who choose not to. It's within our attitude we tap into and place demand on our potential as given to us from God. Our attitude is shaped and developed by what we hear. We are to take care how we listen and who we are listening to. As shown in Luke 8:16–18, if we are listening to the voices of the ministry gifts God has sent to us, there will be a revealing of the things God has hidden in us.

It is vital we develop the attitude of faith because the things God has hidden inside of us will only relate to the world around us through our believing. Paul told the Thessalonians that their faith has sounded out to the world beyond Macedonia and Achaia. God desires our agreement, not our compliance, and it is only through faith we can enter into agreement with Him. This is where hearing the Word of God becomes so important. When we receive from what God is saying to us, we also receive an impartation from that Word.

As our mind is renewed in the thoughts and ways of God, we begin to walk with Him with our focus on things heavenly, not on things earthly. This transitions us from compliance to agreement. The Bible asks the question in Amos 3:3: "How can two walk together unless they are in agreement?" The act of compliance suggests we are doing something because it is expected of us or commanded of us. Agreement suggests we are doing something because we share the same interests and considerations on the subject. This is the reason the multitude came to hear Jesus and receive healing in Luke 6:17–19.

Looking into this portion of scripture, we notice the act of hearing would come before the act of healing. It is an established fact that faith comes as we hear from the Word of God. This created the climate and environment of faith because what they heard brought them into agreement with the desires of the Father. They came that day with their bodies pilfered by sickness, disease, oppression, and hopelessness. Yet as they listened to Jesus teaching them, the things that seemed impossible now appeared possible. Based upon what they heard, the whole multitude was full of faith to touch Him because their touch of faith and agreement was releasing the healing power of God. The Bible says that they all were healed because of the environment of faith, which provides a path for the power of God to flow.

Let's notice something else about this environment charged with faith and healing. The scripture says that power was coming out from Jesus and into them as they touched Him. The climate for miracles became so strong that all received healing. This phenomenon occurred because an environment suitable for an invasion of the heavenly allowed the habitation of God to become intertwined with the earthly. There are those who would say that this happened because God wanted it to. Well, if that is the case, something became disconnected at Nazareth because He obviously went into His hometown with the intention of doing mighty miracles.

I have seen and experienced the heart of God, which displays His overwhelming love for us, demonstrating His affluent desire that He always wants to minister miracles. For the power of God to encompass a multitude of that nature, there was a climactic event producing an environment of agreement for the healing and delivering power to flow from Jesus to them.

In Mark 5, we see another crowd trying to access this same power without the environment. The woman with the issue of blood disease must have heard about this teaching from Jesus. She positioned herself to touch Jesus, and upon her touch of faith, power went out from Jesus in the same manner and healed her. Jesus stopped where he stood, looked at His disciples, and responded, "Someone touched me. " Peter, who was being tossed around while trying to keep Jesus from being thronged by the crowd, replied, "The crowd is pressing on you to touch you, and you say somebody touched me?" Jesus said, "Power has gone out from me."

The woman came and told Jesus everything, and Jesus told her that her faith had made her whole. She received from Jesus through the touch of faith, yet there isn't any mention that anyone else was healed although a multitude was pressing Him. What was the difference? It had to be what she heard about Jesus and mixing what she heard with a response of faith. This placed her in agreement with the flow of His anointing to heal her of the disease that had plagued her for twelve years. The others who were around Jesus were reacting to a possibility that if they did what others had done, they would receive from Him as well. However, their touch was not because of what they heard about Him but what their need was. This also is a stark illustration of what happened in Luke 6 with the multitude. They were pressing him just like this, but there was an atmosphere of agreement. These stories illustrate to us the willingness of God to exercise His power in accordance with an attitude to believe, which exhibits agreement. Our faith moves us into agreement with God.

THE FOURTH TRUTH IS WORSHIP

The fourth truth I want us to look at is found in Matthew 15:21–28 as written in the New American Standard Bible. It is the truth concerning worship. God is looking for those people who will worship Him in spirit and truth. As we read this scripture, keep in mind that she must create an environment of faith for God to operate in.

> Jesus went away from there, and withdrew into the district of Tyre and Sidon. And a Canaanite woman from that region came out and began to cry out, saying, "Have mercy on me, Lord, Son of David; my daughter is cruelly demon-possessed." But He did not answer her. And His disciples came and implored Him, saying, "Send her away, because she keeps shouting at us." But He answered and said, "I was sent only to the lost sheep of the house of Israel." But she came and began to bow down before Him, saying, "Lord, help me!" And He answered and said, "It is not good to take the children's bread and throw it to the dogs." But she said, "Yes, Lord; but even the dogs feed on the crumbs which fall from their masters' table." Then Jesus said to her, "O woman, your faith is great; it shall be done for you as you wish." And her daughter was healed at once.

This is a story about a mother who is a Canaanite woman. She has annoyed the disciples continually, crying out for an audience with Jesus. Her cry of faith is the same as that which Bartimaeus shouted out. Like him she believes Jesus to be the Christ; however, unlike him, she is not a Jew and is therefore disqualified from the benefits of God's salvation for Israel. Her persistence is to be commended, but Jesus refuses to stop and listen to her. Mercy will not overstep justice; however, the communion of true worship will. While her cry of faith did not get the Lord's attention, her worship declaring her faith did. When she bowed herself in worship, she created an environment for Jesus to engage her. After some dialogue, Jesus told this Canaanite mother that her faith was great, and it shall be done for her as she desired. Take note of the connection between her worship and her faith. She came to Jesus in faith, believing He could and would set her daughter free. Her worship was an extension of her overwhelming confidence in that which she had heard about Jesus. Her daughter was set free at that very moment.

Another incident of praise changing the climate and creating an environment for God's power is in Acts 16:22–34. Paul and Silas were thrown into the inner prison there in Philippi, and at midnight, the prisoners were listening to them, praying and singing praise to God. Suddenly, a great earthquake shook the foundations of the prison house, and immediately all the doors were opened and everyone's chains were unfastened. The environment and climate of bondage became that which is suitable for freedom, salvation, and liberty because of prayer and praise.

I want to take this a step further, discussing the seraphim of Isaiah 6:1–4. The scripture says Isaiah saw the Lord in a vision sitting on a throne, lofty and exalted. Verse 2 tells us he also saw seraphim standing above Him. I want you to notice the position of these seraphim as being above the throne. They are positioned there as a covering. We read on to verse 3, noticing they are calling out one to another. They are verbalizing something they heard and/or saw as they communed with the One sitting on the throne. Their words as Isaiah heard it declared a worshipful accolade of "Holy is the Lord of Hosts" while they proclaimed, "The whole earth is full of His glory."

We see and hear from Isaiah's account a heavenly activity occurring. From what we know and realize in Jesus' prayer that it is the Father's desire that the heavenly be duplicated in the earth. This is where we must realize the culture and environment of heaven. Faith is certainly a constant in this account, so to say the seraphim are speaking words of faith and revelation is an understatement. As they are calling out to one another, they are releasing the purpose of the Father into the earth. The result of their words is found in verse 4. Isaiah witnessed the foundations of the thresholds shaking and trembling at the voice of Him who called out while the temple was filling with smoke.

God used the covering agents of heaven to create and release something from His innermost desire. They did this as they spoke from revelation and worship. We also see in verses 3 and 4 that what was spoken in heaven carried the weight of the earth because Isaiah heard them say "The whole earth is full of His glory."

Upon the resurrection of Jesus from the dead, we know He was highly exalted above every name and being. The passage of Hebrews 1:2 tells us that in these days, God speaks to us in and through His Son. I want to submit to you that now Jesus has received honor and exaltation being positioned as the Lord of the covering. Whatever the Father's desire, it is released as it flows from the Lord Jesus Christ. Jesus said in John 16:15,

"All things that the Father has are mine. Therefore I said that He will take of mine and reveal it to you."

This revelation and worship flows through us into the earth, bringing about powerful demonstrations of His Presence. These demonstrations employ the angels of God, and they go to work creating the climate, environment, and culture of heaven in the earth. As we yield to the mind of the Spirit, we witness the climate and environment of faith bringing about the manifestation of God's glory.

THE WORD OF HIS POWER

As we consider the connection between faith and the working of God's mighty power, it is appropriate we take a look into two events that happened in the lives of Christ's disciples during the His earthly ministry. We want to examine how the power of God flows like electricity along the path of words that are spoken from someone's faith. The Apostle Paul spoke of God's power as exceedingly great and connected it to the resurrection power, which raised Jesus from the dead. He said in Ephesians 1:19 that this power flows toward us who believe, and in Hebrews 1:3 it is said that Jesus upholds all things by the Word of His Power. In John 7:38–39, Jesus used the analogy of rushing waters as in a swollen river to describe the power of God's Spirit flowing through us. Jesus describes the Holy Spirit as the Spirit of Truth, and in John 17, He identifies the Word as Truth. This reveals to us the absolute connection between the person, work, and power of the Holy Spirit and the Word of God. With this we

discover that the power of God flows along the path of
words spoken from our faith.

There are two events in the gospels I want us to
consider concerning this truth. The first event in the lives
of the disciples I want us to look at is the multiplication
of the loaves and fish we find in Matthew 14. In fact,
this miracle is the only account of Jesus' ministry that
is presented to us in all four gospels. This event is so
important to understanding His miraculous power
that Jesus refers to it as a key to understanding and
comprehending truths related to the manifestation of
heaven's authority, force, and strength. The scripture
in Mark 6:52 tell us that the disciples were to gain
insight from the incident of the loaves. This event
demonstrates the exchange between His words and the
manifest power of the Father. Let's survey this miracle
as presented in all four gospels.

There is a great multitude that most historians
estimate to be at least fifteen thousand people. These
people had been with Jesus all day, and it was now
approaching evening, probably around four in the
afternoon. The disciples recognize the necessity of
sending the crowds away in order for them to get to
neighboring farms and villages to find food and lodging.
Being in such a remote place left them without access
to these things.

Another thing to notice here is Jesus is mindful of
the physical and nutritional needs of the multitude. He
is interested in meeting the needs of people regardless
of how minor or great they may be. Three of the four
gospels tell us that Jesus commissioned the disciples

to give them something to eat. He knew the only resources present were a little boy's lunch consisting of five biscuits and two sardines. Yet Jesus' word carried the power necessary for the disciples to do what He said and participate in possibly the greatest miracle of Jesus ministry.

As we notice Jesus' intent to feed the multitudes, we also take note that He wasn't limited to the supply of resources or circumstances around Him. He knew the Father possessed all the power needed to fulfill the purpose set forth through words spoken from faith.

Because we are familiar with how electricity is utilized in our homes and everyday lives, we can see some truth to this miracle through considering the laws of electricity. The electricity coming into the building is virtually unlimited. Its power is regulated by the breaker box through which it flows to access points throughout the structure. Each access point then supplies certain amperage of electricity for use. It can be used as long as there is a demand placed upon it.

This is just like the power of God. As it flows into our lives, it is virtually unlimited. The power is regulated through our faith in His Word. Our words spoken from faith become access points from which people can receive from the power of God according to what they believe.

I remember an incident in my ministry where some people were healed without me even touching them. As I was preaching and teaching on the subject of grace and miracles, I was moved to say that someone present with hearing problems could be healed if they would believe what the Word of God is saying about the subject. This woman stood up spontaneously and cried out she could hear out of her left ear.

There was a man there who came running forward to the front of the audience holding the left side of his head. He was screaming and crying all at the same time. Some pastors who were present met him at the front and asked him what was going on as they calmed him down. He told them that he was a war veteran, and he had been injured, destroying his inner ear along with his eardrum, and he had been deaf in that ear since then. When he heard what I said by the Spirit, he mixed faith in God's Word for his healing, saying, "I believe I receive." As he was thanking God for his hearing, a miracle manifested in his body. He could hear perfectly well out of an ear that had been destroyed.

Another man in that same meeting was standing off to my left, and he raised his hand to get someone's attention as they were getting this other man's testimony. One of the pastors went over to him, and this man told of a childhood accident that destroyed his inner ear. The surgeon had to remove his eardrum. He too had mixed his faith with the power of God present and experienced a manifestation of healing and miracles.

In this same service, a woman with a severe condition in her back, which was the result of a car accident, could not straighten up and was in severe pain. She too mixed faith in God's Word for her life at the time the power of God was present and received healing and restoration for her back. She was jumping up and down, demonstrating her freedom and mobility.

Hallelujah! All of these testimonies occurred at the same time as they plugged into the words I spoke concerning a release of God's power.

Now I want to mention something here. I was moved by the Spirit to say what I did, and the power of God manifested. You cannot just go around doing this as you see the need or as you just decide to. Jesus did and spoke what He heard and saw from His Father. Even so should we operate like this, and we will see the results He saw.

As there are various appliances that use electricity, the appliance itself determines the manifestation of the electricity used. The electricity that enables the stove to produce heat for cooking is the same power that gives the refrigerator or freezer the ability to cool or freeze its contents. There isn't any distinction in the power; the difference is found in the purpose and application of the appliance placing demand on the power. In this same way, faith gives manifestation and interpretation to God's unlimited power. This is the lesson of the loaves. When they were full, the multiplication anointing waned, and by the time the anointing lifted, there were twelve baskets of fragments left over.

The second event in the lives of the disciples I want us to look at is the miracle of Peter walking on the water to go to Jesus. It's one thing to grasp the reality that Jesus walked on a stormy sea, but it is another thing to embrace the fact that Peter walked on the same water to go to Jesus. This event happened after the crowds were sent away as they had finished eating from what resembled an all-you-can-eat buffet of fish and bread.

Jesus had given the disciples direction to go to the other side. The only way across was by boat, and as they were on their way, a storm came upon the body of water. The wind was blowing contrary to them, and they could not make any headway. It was about midnight when they saw Jesus walking toward them on the water.

It was Peter who spoke to Jesus. There was a question whether it was really him or not, so Peter knew that if it was really him, he could speak a word for him to come, and the same power holding Jesus up would enable Peter to do the same. Jesus said one word, and Peter climbed out of the boat and, upon the meaning and power of that one word, lived the miraculous. The lesson of the loaves to be learned and applied here is that Jesus told them to go to the other side. If they had considered the miracle of the loaves, they would have gone straight over regardless of the storm, operating in the miracle power of Jesus' words just as they did feeding the multitude. John's gospel tells us that as soon as Jesus entered the boat, they were immediately on the shore of the other side. This is the outcome the Lord intended when He spoke to them to travel across the water to the other shore.

In reviewing this event, we can conclude the absolute agreement between the Word as truth and the Spirit of Truth. Jesus upholds all things by the Word of His Power. As the Word of God enters into our heart and we have understanding of that Word, there becomes a providential environment for the power of God to be manifested through us. We will operate within the authority of His resurrection as we speak what we believe. My experience is that we can't help but speak from the authority of God's power because faith translates out of our spirit into our mouths. When the words of faith are spoken, the agencies of heaven go into motion, bringing manifestation of those words. It may come to pass immediately, and then it may not.

As words of faith are considered seeds of the Kingdom, there are those occasions that the season of harvest must come to maturity before there is the full realization of the promise declared through faith. However, you can be sure as Abraham was that it will surely come to pass. Remember in Matthew's gospel when Jesus spoke to the fig tree, and it dried up from the roots? It was the next day before Peter realized what had happened and called to mind the event of Jesus cursing this tree. Just a side note, Jesus did not speak death to the tree; He said that there wouldn't be any fruit to grow upon it from that day forward. He removed the tree's purpose, and death set in.

We must be sensitive to the mind of God as He wants us to remember that He is our sufficiency. I could share with you story after story about this fact; however, I will point you to God's Word. The Roman centurion said to Jesus, "Speak the word concerning healing to my servant, and he shall be healed." The hemorrhaging woman said, "If I may touch his garment, I too shall be made whole."

The royal official in John 4 believed the word that Jesus spoke concerning his son and went his way with no apparent evidence. We all know he was rehearsing the words he heard from Jesus as he travelled home.

When those of his household met him on the road, I'm sure he was not surprised to hear the news they brought him. The father learned of the timing of his son's healing and knew it occurred the previous day when he believed what Jesus spoke to him. God's faithfulness, power, and presence are readily available to all who will believe, and this is faith's reward.

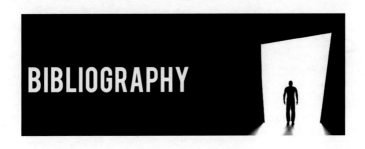

BIBLIOGRAPHY

Lester Sumrall, *The Gifts and Ministries of the Holy Spirit*, (New Kensington, PA: Whitaker House Publishing, 1982).